COLLISION

Theory vs. Reality in Expert Systems

COLLISION

Theory vs. Reality in Expert Systems

Second Edition

Lawrence K. Laswell

QED Information Sciences, Inc.
Wellesley, Massachusetts

P.O. Box 181
Wellesley, MA 02181

Library of Congress Catalog Number: 89-3723
International Standard Book Number: 0-89435-294-6

Printed in the United States of America
89 90 91 10 9 8 7 6 5 4 3 2 1

Library of Congress Cataloging-in-Publication Data

Laswell, Lawrence K.
Collision : theory vs. reality in expert systems / Lawrence K. Laswell.
p. cm.
ISBN 0-89435-294-6
1. Expert systems (Computer science) I. Title.
QA76.76.E95L37 1989
006.3'3—dc19

Thanks to:

Alvena
Bill
Carl
Christy
John
Tom
Toni

and

Barb who kept the coffee hot.

Contents

Section III – The Technology

Section IV – Development

Index to Illustrations

Preface

Expert systems have been marketed as a new and different technology that cannot and should not be treated like other computer disciplines. During the introduction of a new technology, it is natural to be skeptical about such claims. Even though this author runs the risk of being hoisted on his own petard, he takes exactly the opposite view. Expert systems are a subdiscipline of software engineering and should be treated as such.

Companies should manage expert systems like any other software and should ignore the hype and resist the seductive nature of the technology.

This does not mean the differences between conventional and expert system software should be ignored. Database software requires the use of special tools, skills and procedures, but these do not dominate software development projects – they coexist with conventional tools and techniques. The same should be true of expert systems.

Regardless of what you may believe about the future of expert systems, expert system programming approaches and techniques are here to stay. The only issue open for debate is what percentage of software in use ten years from now will be expert system software. When it comes time to introduce expert systems to your organization, do it right. Start out with modest, doable objectives that produce business benefit. Invest in the proper skills and training and don't get caught in analysis-paralysis or toy-building – do something that makes a difference.

Section I

Management Considerations

cost justification structure is presented that links the technology, system development, and business objectives.

Market Viewpoints

Expert systems belong to a family of technologies collectively referred to as *artificial intelligence* or simply *AI*. The artificial intelligence market is greatly confused and it is easy to be misled by vendors and the trade press. The generic nature of the technology is partly to blame because there are so many ways to view the technology. In this environment, it is important to keep the many viewpoints in their proper context. An individual's view of AI can be influenced by his education, industry, or application focus. Views can also be influenced by the four major voices in the AI marketplace: academic, marketing, military, and business. In the October 1986 issue of VENTURE, William Logan stated the problem succinctly.

> "To academics, AI is an Anything Impossible; to marketers, Anything Interesting; to the Department of Defense, Anything Invincible; and to civilian users, Anything Improved."

Academics

At the origin of the technology, research scientists are working to expand the frontiers of computer science. The perspective of the research scientist is of particular importance. AI is still more of a dream than it is a technology. The very act of defining a dream limits the vision, and kills the dream. As the guardians of the technology, the scientists must protect it. It may be an overstatement but to them, anything that works has reached definition and represents a step forward, but is no longer AI. For example, voice synthesis ceased to be AI once it left the lab. In development, an expert system is an AI development project, but when done, the AI community rarely recognizes the system as an example of artificial intelligence.

The AI technologist is concerned about future possibilities, not present capabilities. In trying to push back the frontiers, researchers have developed methodologies to prove capability. This is quite different from delivering capability and explains why research and business software management approaches differ substantially.

For years, the AI community was dominated by the research perspective and essentially remained a closed society. Those who knew AI, or those trained by the AI community, were the only spokesmen for the technology. As a result, most literature reflected this limited research perspective. By lacking business crystallization and pragmatic expression, these communications have led to confusion and misunderstanding.

Marketing

The Madison Avenue marketing gurus quickly understood the sales implications of AI since public interest has given AI a measure of marketing top spin. Salesmen found that just the mention of AI would quickly open previously closed doors. Marketing personnel created pseudo AI by simply relabeling their products as AI to provide valuable product differentiation in crowded or confused markets. Toasters had AI because they were smart enough not to burn

the toast. Telephone answering machines had AI because they could answer the phone and talk. Televisions had AI because they had intelligent circuits capable of locking on to the incoming signal. Some computer systems suddenly became AI systems just because they could make decisions.

The hype has led to perceptions that have wrongly valued the technology, added confusion, and created misunderstanding. In the current market environment caveat emptor applies to vendors, consultants, and internal staffs.

Military

The flow of government money was the sustaining lifeblood for the early AI industry growth. For years, the lion's share of AI money flowed from the Pentagon. Invincibility is expensive: military systems need to be effective and cost is a distant secondary concern. Huge sums of military money helped shape the technology and the effects are still evident today. In 1983, a businessman attending an AI user meeting commented he was the only one there using the technology for non-lethal purposes. The focus was on researching huge, complex, and highly technical applications for which delivery to end users is a foreign concept. For better or for worse, military funding sheltered the AI community and allowed it to stand apart from mainstream data processing.

Business

Today Logan's civilian, the business manager, is simply looking for a way to improve operations. The business manager, unable to relate to theoretical or

military applications and under a marketing siege, is at a disadvantage. The manager wants pragmatic, candid, present-tense answers to the What, Why, How, and Where of the technology.

Artificial Intelligence

The term *artificial intelligence* is an oxymoron. Not only contradictory, it implies something that does not exist. Be that as it may, the term is commonly used and must be dealt with before moving on to expert systems.

A working definition of artificial intelligence is: "A research area focused on producing machines exhibiting behaviors normally associated with human intelligence." Since intelligence is the common denominator in the seeing, hearing, speaking, moving, grasping, and thinking processes, artificial intelligence must encompass them.

Thus, artificial intelligence is an umbrella term that is used to describe a broad array of technologies directed towards machine emulation of human behaviors. Each technology is still the subject of research and each is in a different stage of commercialization. Sometimes, AI and expert systems are confused and it becomes difficult to separate one from the other. The differences are important because what is true of AI as a whole may not be true of the individual technologies and vice versa.

Science fiction is rich with man-like machines, robots, or androids exhibiting near-human behavior and fact often follows fiction. These human-like

machines would be able to see, hear, speak, move, think, and grasp objects. Separate scientific research concentrated on each of these facets has produced its own technology: seeing – machine vision; hearing – voice recognition; speaking – voice synthesis; moving and grasping – robotics; and thinking – expert systems. Individually, each technology is AI; collectively they are AI. The definition depends on context.

The human body and mind are complex, interrelated systems and any endeavor to replicate them can be expected to be equally complex and interrelated. This fact is partly to blame for the layman's confusion about the definition of artificial intelligence. For example, it is of little use for a machine to see an object unless it understands what it sees and can do something with it. Consequently, machine vision systems often include robotics and expert systems. Research into handwriting recognition can include machine learning, expert systems, and vision. Once capable of recognizing individual letters and words, systems must extract the intelligence from the written word with natural language processing. A complete artificial intelligence system is still the subject of fiction and would be the functional equivalent of R2-D2 or C3PO, the droids from the movie *Star Wars*.

AI: The Long View

The long term impact of AI will be profound. Current research is directed at producing technology that will ultimately lead to a radically different business world. What impact would these capabilities have on the office environment?

- Data entry does not require human intervention. Data entry methods include voice via telephone and the typed or handwritten page via scanners. The data entry system is capable of handling free-form service or information requests.

- After entry, the system automatically indexes and routes information for disposition.

- Knowledgeable software automatically handles most, if not all, routine tasks from start to finish.

- Users communicate with computer systems in plain English by voice, keyboard, or electronic tablet.

- User interfaces are highly sophisticated. The information supplied to the user varies in content and structure depending on the task.

Capabilities such as these spark imagination and are responsible for the enthusiasm and excitement surrounding the AI. If these revolutionary capabilities existed today in a commercially viable form, they would change our view of computers, and organizations would change to adapt to the technology. However, these capabilities, although technically possible, will not be viable for some years to come. The gulf separat-

ing possibility and viability is caused by lack of integration, high cost, and technical immaturity. The gulf has been made to appear smaller than it really is because of the many confusing voices in the marketplace.

Expert Systems

Expert systems, concentrating on the organization and thought processes of the human mind, comes under the artificial intelligence umbrella. In recent years, business has given expert systems the most attention. Because of the attention, expert system technology is beginning to take on its own identity. To some this means that AI *is* expert systems. To others, it means expert systems no longer belong to AI.

Expert systems are difficult to define in nontechnical terms because they employ a diverse set of software techniques. For discussion, the techniques can be divided into two categories: people-oriented and software-oriented. Knowledge acquisition refers to the people-oriented techniques used in acquiring, defining, and specifying knowledge. The software-related tasks include the actual program design, coding, and testing. In its common connotation, the term knowledge engineering is used to define both the people-oriented and software-oriented tasks.

The software techniques for knowledge representation, rule construction, and inferencing control, which will be explained in later chapters, are the distinguishing characteristics of expert system software. Expert systems can also use any number of sophisticated mathematical modeling techniques to handle uncertainty and probability. However, a system is not an expert system just because it uses these techniques any more than it is an expert system just by virtue of its decision-making capability. Likewise, a system is not an expert system because it was built by a person with the Knowledge Engineering job title. Expert systems are defined here as software built using rule-inferencing (RI) software techniques that are explained in later chapters. The rule-inferencing definition was chosen because it is the characteristic that makes expert systems unique.

One more comment about terminology. The term *expert system* is as bad as *artificial intelligence* and unfortunately is emotionally charged with connotations that both inspire and threaten. The term also implies and promises something that does not exist. The term *expert* as used in the AI community refers to an individual with eight to ten years of experience and education. This narrow definition would effectively eliminate the vast majority of potential business applications. At the opposite extreme, if taken too broadly the term could imply that any system capable of decisions or analysis is an *expert* system.

In the commercial world, with a few rare exceptions, *expert* systems do not exist. Systems do exist with modules or components built using expert system techniques that can assist and support the human decision process. If we avoid debate over the definition of *expert*, and use its common connotation, systems rarely achieve an *expert* level of performance. *Knowledge system* is a better term, however both will be used interchangeably.

Applications

Expert systems represent a valuable general-purpose technology that can be applied to an infinite variety of applications ranging from small personal computer programs to large complex systems. Expert systems applications can be divided into four groups, each varying by size, as depicted in Figure 1.1.

The top layer of the cube contains applications that require little or no integration with conventional computer systems and data files. For reasons that will be discussed in later chapters, most existing applications

Figure 1.1 – Expert System Application Cube

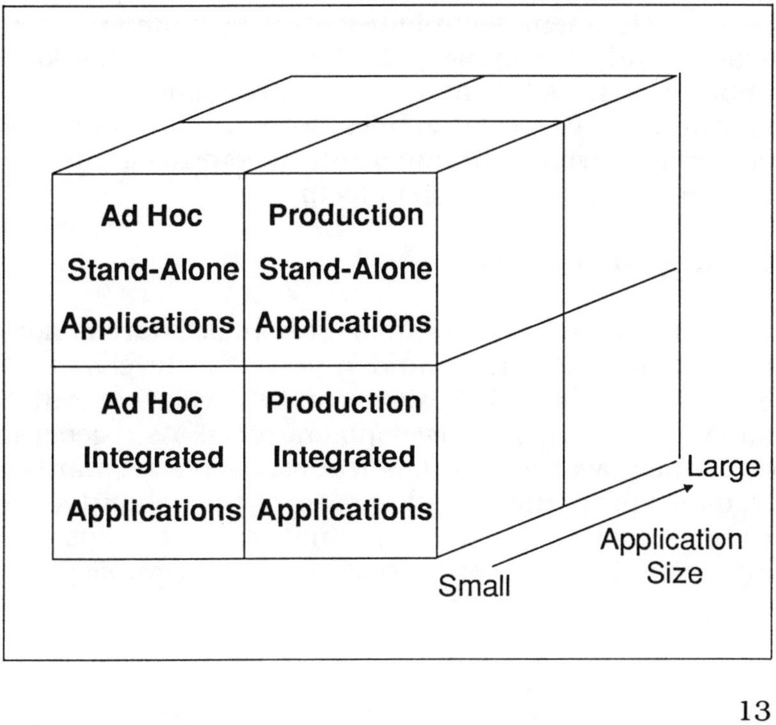

fall into this category. Most recent office applications fall into the bottom row. These commercial integrated systems are recognized as the wave of the future.

The left column contains applications designed for users who need help periodically on an ad hoc basis. These applications are not intended for use in a production environment which requires users to use the application as an integral part of their day-to-day jobs.

Expert systems were born with applications in the large, stand-alone, ad hoc portion of the cube. In these classic applications, the spotlight is on technology, elegance of solution, and the power of the development tools. These applications have long been the grist of the research community since they represent the greatest technical challenge. Most popular expert system development techniques are the product of research and development of these large, stand-alone applications. In this area, integration issues and conventional software practices were understandably viewed as trivial or unimportant in comparison to the challenges of expert system technology.

Development Tools

To build an expert system, special software is normally required to assist and support the development effort. The required software can be special computer languages, or hybrid development tools. As a general rule, the power and sophistication of this software is in direct proportion to the power of the computer on which it was designed to run. In turn, the size, power, and cost of the computer used to run the application is indicative of the application size. Because of this, the application size shown in Figure 1.1 refers to both the size of the software tool and the computer used.

Unfortunately for some, the technology and techniques developed have become more a matter of theology rather than just one way to view a large, diverse, and complex universe of applications. More unfortunate still is the fact that these views have been reinforced in the popular trade press, literature, and dialogue on expert systems. Through constant reinforcement, theory and viewpoints have become immutable facts that serve only to reinforce the theology.

In this respect, the AI community has been its own worst enemy in the battle to get expert systems accepted by the business community where integration and productivity are the cornerstones of modern computer systems. The characteristics of integrated production systems are as different from the classical expert systems as expert systems are from conventional software. From a business perspective, the elegance, the size, and the "smarts" of the system are not nearly as important as usability and return on investment.

Expert systems are a valuable tool that can be used in innumerable ways. Intelligence or expertise is not a prerequisite – expert systems can be used as a programmer productivity tool to develop conventional applications dependent on highly complex logic trees. Expensive and exotic hardware and software are not required – many useful applications have been built using simple, low-cost personal computer software that does not require specialized skills and training.

In subsequent chapters, the four quadrants of the application cube are explored and contrasted with each other and conventional software. The exploration reveals that the tale of expert systems is a treble tale of two worlds: conventional versus AI software, stand-alone versus integrated applications, and small versus large applications.

2

Expectations

Until companies become familiar with the development and use of expert systems, the first step in every project will be to find a problem to solve with expert systems, rather than letting the business need select the technology. This is natural problem for any emerging technology and is caused by the business community's lack of familiarity with the new technology. But unlike most other technologies, expert systems must overcome expectation-setting stereotypes caused by overselling. Dismantling some of these expectations is the necessary first step in identifying realistic business opportunities.

Stereotypes

In its infancy, the AI community considered the discussion of IBM mainframes an act of heresy. As recently as 1986, expert system vendors were still enchanted with exotic hardware and complex technical applications. Since then, the vendors have done an about-face. They have addressed the three biggest commercial barriers: integration, cost, and performance. Unfortunately, the flow of information has not kept pace.

It is still difficult for companies to accumulate actionable information on business applications. Some see this as continuing evidence of immaturity. The paucity of information is troubling, but does not imply lack of success. Many applications attract little or no attention, and companies will say precious little about their successes. Possibly, small applications don't seem newsworthy, or perhaps companies see no reason to educate the competition. Whatever the reason, most information flows from vendors or researchers who lack a business application perspective. Unfortunately, without that perspective the vendors cannot be effective in communicating their successes and overcoming past stereotypes.

In past years, exotic hardware was the main barrier to commercial acceptance. Because of incompatibility with standard computers, several technically successful systems never made it to production. Vendors are rapidly putting this problem behind them by delivering sophisticated software compatible with mainstream equipment. Depending on the vendor, companies can now select from a veritable cafeteria of computer options.

In addition to the mainframe tools, many personal computer tools are available. Previously associated with small or toy applications, personal computer tools have grown substantially. For example, a major auditing firm developed a serious personal computer application consisting of 6,000 rules divided among 31 knowledge bases. Used by auditors nationwide, the system analyzes commercial loans.

Companies often cite the technology's high cost as a barrier. Although costs are coming down, this problem still deserves discussion. Current cost information applies to initial development projects. Having to bear start-up and learning costs, initial development efforts are more expensive than later ones. Also, a major component of past start-up costs included specialized computer hardware which is rapidly becoming passé.

The most important part of the expense question is one of scale. The bigger the application the higher the cost. Many useful inexpensive applications have been fielded but unfortunately, large applications gain the most attention.

Expert systems are typecast as slow plodding creatures incapable of handling high-volume office applications. What is true of complex technical applications isn't necessarily true of simpler office applications. Performance improvements and careful design have produced impressive production systems.

The dialogue required to erase market perceptions built in the early days is sparse. This is partly because the companies leading in expert system use see these systems as strategic advantage and want to keep their existence secret. However, in the latter part of 1987 an interesting trend began. A few companies were forced into expert system development as a defensive measure to offset the competitive advantage the technology had given their competition. Competition is a powerful force in the marketplace and will help speed commercialization.

Myths

Expertise

It is unfortunate that expert systems have become associated with applications that require expertise because this association can limit the potential application of expert systems. Tasks that required an expert level of competence were traditionally the target of expert system applications in the late seventies and early eighties. If expert systems were used only for tasks that require an *expert*, most potential business applications would be eliminated.

One standard selection criteria for expert system applications is that expertise be present and that expertise be nonuniformly distributed. A better way to look at expertise is to view it as a matter of employee competence in a given task. An employee's competence can be a matter of intelligence and personal skills as well as training, knowledge, or experience. Expert systems cannot do anything about the employee's native abilities, but they can help in areas where competence is a function of time.

The bar chart in Figure 2.1 plots the relative performance of employees grouped by length of experience. This chart would normally be associated with tasks that do not require expertise, since competence does not appear to depend on the length of experience as is shown in Figure 2.2. When performance

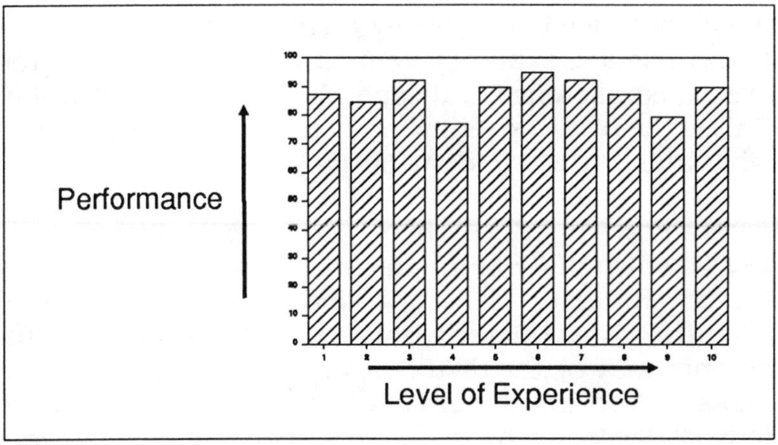

Figure 2.1 – Performance not Dependent on Experience

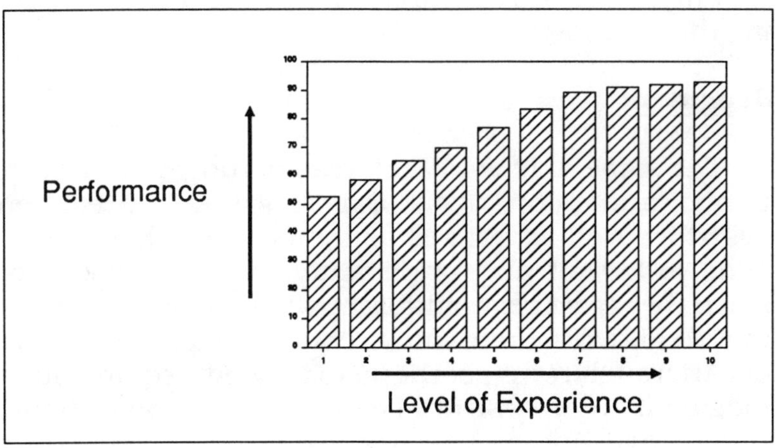

Figure 2.2 – Performance Dependent on Experience

or competence is not evenly distributed by location or by experience, expert systems can be used to raise the overall competence and capability of the organization. This is the primary selling point for expert systems, but what about uniform distribution?

Uniform distribution of competence is normally used to disqualify an application as an expert system target. However, this may overlook several potential benefits. An apparent uniform distribution of competence may be the result of severely time-constrained tasks, a good training program, a mature organization, low employee turnover, low overall productivity, or very simple tasks. Expert systems probably can't help with very simple tasks, but they can be used to decompress decision times, improve productivity, and immunize organizations against employee turnover. If uniform performance distribution is the result of a solid training program, expert systems can also help by reducing the amount of formal training or by constantly reinforcing the training material.

Judgment

The same is true in the areas of judgment, uncertainty, and heuristics. Expert systems are often described and advertised as systems capable of handling judgment and uncertainty, but that does not mean they can't be profitably applied elsewhere. Tasks that require research, intelligent information retrieval, or a thorough review of the facts may not require much judgment but may be ideal expert system applications.

Impressiveness

Individuals who are waiting to see an expert system demonstration that dazzles the eye and boggles the mind are in for a long, long wait. As a society we have become blasé about computer technology. Rarely will we see something done by a computer that astounds us because we have been conditioned to expect a great deal from computers. We are much more likely to be impressed by the way a computer program was designed, or by the care and craftsmanship that went into its construction. So if we are amazed by an expert system application, it probably will be the craftsmanship that got our attention, not the technology.

Most business computer systems are dull, boring, relentless, reliable, and consistent workhorses that get the job done. They are hardly the type of thing we are likely to get excited about. To expect anything different from expert systems is a mistake because most business applications shun the glitz-graphics-and-flash media image created for them. They are deceptively unimpressive, and because they are incapable of out-smarting or out-thinking users they are non-threatening. After running a test case through an expert system, an expert is likely to be unimpressed and say, "So what, I could have told you that." If the system was well designed, the analysis and reasoning of the system will appear quite simple and straightforward. The magic some individuals are looking for is not directly apparent. The magic, if any exists at all, is that the system could bore the expert a thousand more times on a thousand different cases.

Interactivity

A common expectation is that an expert system will be highly interactive, look different, and behave different than conventional systems. Part of this expectation is based on media fixation with large workstation-based stand-alone ad hoc applications, and part is based on our conventional system experiences and expectations. None of these expectations are necessarily correct.

Stand-alone PC applications are usually highly interactive and can be expected to look and feel new. However, most production or integrated systems in use look like any other conventional application, because the expert system is encapsulated in a substantial layer of conventional software. Most demonstrations of expert systems are based on a dialogue-intensive user interface (dialogue here can either be verbal or a user-computer dialogue based on graphics, icons, selection bars, etc.) that resembles a game of "twenty questions." To date, the most common use of expert systems is for ad hoc applications. These applications are not used in production eight hours a day, five days a week and are employed to help users or provide some service.

Because they are performing ad hoc duties where expertise is the primary concern, productivity is not an issue. Such systems can effectively use dialogue-oriented user interfaces to question the user about the problem until enough information is gleaned to provide the advice sought.

Production applications seldom require the users to carry on a conversation with their computer – expert system or not, production application interfaces are streamlined, straightforward, and built for speed, not elegance.

On-Line Applications

On-line computer system expectations are similar to the interactivity expectations. We have become accustomed to on-line applications with one- or two-second response times. Our expectation is that any new technology should be at least as good. This is a yardstick problem for expert systems and is an apples and oranges comparison. Because of their inferencing characteristics, expert systems can be computer intensive, slowing response times and/or slowing all other applications to a crawl.

Expert systems are not transaction processing systems and often the nature of the task does not require instantaneous response. Expert systems do not have to be real-time. This is a difficult concept for both users and technologists to understand. Users are accustomed to instantaneous update and the technologists see their technology defined as real-time and interactive. Despite these expectations, several companies have found that applications do not need to be real-time and a recent survey showed that 22% of applications in use were executed in batch. By using expert systems in a batch mode, they have found they can achieve most of the benefits and eliminate response time worries.

Common Sense

Common sense deserves special mention because the term is misused in conjunction with expert systems and can cause companies to miss possible opportunities. For years, we have been told expert systems can't handle common sense. Understandably then, some potential applications are dismissed because the user claims there is nothing magic about his/her job – it is just common sense. If this were truly correct, there would be no difference between beginners and experienced personnel. Usually what has happened is the user has developed some expertise, and through repetition and experience the job becomes second nature. However, when asked for an example of common sense, they reply with a statement like the one below.

> "It is common sense that you don't issue life insurance to someone who is terminally ill. Everyone knows that."

Even though the statement seems like common sense it is actually a basic rule that could be placed in an expert system as shown below.

If Applicant is Terminally Ill
THEN
Don't Issue the Policy.

Common sense as used in the AI community relates to the holistic fusion of our consciousness, life experiences, sensory input, and knowledge. If the research community ever precisely defines common sense, expert systems probably won't be able to support it. However, in the meantime, basic task knowledge should not be confused with common sense.

3
Applications

There are three things to consider in discussing expert system applications: how the system is used, what it is used for, and what its primary focus is. Each of these areas – usage, application, and focus – deserve attention.

Usage

The application cube introduced in Chapter 1 represents one usage model for expert systems. Internal to each of the eight application areas, systems can be built that differ in the user-system relationship and the system's level of autonomy.

Assistant and Mentor

Functionally, an expert system can act as an intelligent assistant that excels at organization and background research. A knowledge base can, in some respects, be considered a library containing facts and rules representing the collective expertise of one or more individuals. In any particular case, only a minuscule fraction of the library is relevant, and some of the information needed may be obscure or lie outside of the user's area of competence. Because expert systems have perfect recall and can use knowledge dynamically, all pertinent information/knowledge can be retrieved, organized, and presented to the user. Depending on the system's purpose, the retrieved knowledge can be displayed as reminders, observations, or recommendations. By performing this function, the system not only provides assistance, it also provides a second opinion and an automated check that nothing is overlooked.

Assistant applications interact with the user by providing automated research, review, and recommendations. Mentor applications differ slightly in that they do not make recommendations, but they do perform the other functions. An assistant system would say, "I recommend . . . because . . . . "; a mentor system would say, "Review these three issues before making a decision because . . . ." Mentor applications are useful if users feel threatened, or if it is impractical to develop a system with the requisite information and/or knowledge.

Autonomy

Completely autonomous applications assimilate information, reason about it, and take action without user intervention. Such applications are rare in business, but semi-autonomous applications have broader application, and can provide substantial productivity improvements. Semi-autonomous systems can either completely handle part of the caseload, or can handle part of each case.

In many tasks, a large percentage of the effort is devoted to reviewing and disposing of standard cases which makes less time available for handling problems.

This is an example of the 80/20 rule where 80% of the effort is devoted to 20% of the problem, and 80% of the problem has to be solved in the remaining 20% of the time. Semi-autonomous expert system applications can prescreen incoming work, handle standard cases, and refer problem cases to users for disposition.

Expert systems can also support review and analysis procedures such as underwriting or loan approval. These procedures generally span several days or weeks and are comprised of many subdecisions and actions that ultimately lead to a final recommendation. Expert systems can be employed to prescreen applications and take autonomous action on many of the smaller subdecisions.

Autonomous and semi-autonomous application only make sense for production or integrated systems. Most stand-alone applications are non-autonomous since they are totally dependent on the user for the final analysis and action.

Applications

Paper and People

When looking for potential expert system applications the best place to start is where, through training and experience, we have been taught not to look – at paper-, form-, and people-intensive tasks. Often, these tasks are those that could not be effectively automated using conventional approaches, and as such are the most fertile area to search for expert system applications. These tasks have not been automated because the information on the forms is not amenable to conventional computer analysis, or the reasoning and logic they require is too complex for conventional computer techniques.

The search should not be limited just to professional tasks; clerical and paraprofessional tasks are also excellent sources for applications. The *expert* focus in expert systems has conditioned us to think only of applications characterized by a few big complex decisions (ad hoc applications). However, those tasks characterized by many small decisions should not be overlooked. Because of the virtues of computer systems, the more mundane and routine a task is, the more amenable it is to automation.

For example, claims processing and underwriting are two dominant applications in the insurance industry. Both are policy guided, paper driven, routine, and highly formalized. The best underwriters and claims adjudicators are those with a command of the facts and the ability to integrate specific problems into the framework of company policy and guidelines.

Troublesome Systems

Conventional computer systems that don't quite measure up to business expectations due to a lack of maintainability, accuracy, capacity, or capability are also good candidates for expert systems, provided the application is decision-like or analysis-like. Programs of this type usually fall into the numerical analysis, statistical, or complex logical categories. Usually these systems were built because a large volume of data needed analysis and it was not cost effective to provide the analysis manually. Often these systems represent a compromise between the way the analysis should be done and the way the computer could do the analysis. Applications that employ a lot of numerical processing just to coax a little intelligence out of a mountain of data can often benefit from an expert system with a little intelligence. This alternative approach may also reduce maintenance costs and produce better results.

Securities trading is a good example. Statistical models exist that attempt to predict future performance based on past statistical trends. However, this represents only half of the equation. Most market analysts will tell you past performance is a relatively poor indicator of future performance. The good market analysts are the "good guessers" who use a complex body of knowledge and judgment that is far beyond statistical modeling. Often these experts require a small amount of diverse data and statistical analysis is seldom a major component in their decision.

In the complex logic category, expert systems can be used as a fourth-generation language for development of these applications. Even though the application will not exhibit the characteristics normally associated with expert systems, the technology can be used to build and maintain such systems. In this way, small but complex applications that were not cost effective using conventional approaches become feasible. At the high end, large complex systems can benefit through lower maintenance and enhancement costs.

Lost Opportunities

Searching for expert systems applications in areas where opportunities were lost in the past is the least obvious area since lost opportunities are not always apparent. Lost opportunities can be a lost sale or service because specialists were mislocated or did not exist, or service took too long or required too much of the customer.

Lost opportunities can also include cost containment. In situations where employees can select from several alternatives that have an associated cost, expert systems can help direct the employee to the least costly alternative.

One company which prided itself on reliability and service had earned a reputation for being able to ship its product virtually anywhere reliably. Much of the reputation relied on one individual who was a walking encyclopedia of shippers, rates, and the best way to get a package to arcane locations. His knowledge was cloned into a system that found the best fit between client needs, reliability, and price. The system, made available to all personnel in the shipping department, allowed the company to maintain service levels but reduce shipping costs while ensuring the experience of the one key employee would never be lost to the company.

Another *lost opportunity* application was a sales assistant for suppliers of electric motors. The system was an intelligent catalog retrieval system capable of interpreting a client's requirements and finding the motor, out of several hundred available, that best met the client's needs. Since sales personnel knowledgeable about all of the motors and applications are rare, some sales were lost if the salesman could not find the right motor in a reasonable amount of time. The system solved the problem by always finding a match if one existed.

Improved Services

Expert systems are being used to improve services by either distributing or replacing expertise. Where services are required at remote locations that require scarce experts or specialists, expert systems can be used to provide the expertise – and hence the service. In some situations, this may allow a company to provide a service it previously could not provide, or make the delivery of the service less awkward or more rapid. Distribution of expertise to improve service is most often accomplished with ad hoc stand-alone applications. Typical applications in this category include financial planning, order completion, tax advice, and product bidding/pricing.

Improved services can be achieved in other situations by electronically replacing the expert in the service cycle. The delivery of some products and services is often delayed due to a review and approval process even though only a fraction of the cases require special expertise. The review is still required, however, because it takes a measure of expertise to identify the special cases. Expert systems can be used in credit approval, contract approval, order assembly, and production scheduling to expedite the review process on standard as well as special cases.

Replacing expertise can also be accomplished in volume overload situations. For example, a company is an information provider and sells its clients evaluations on thousands of items. Even though all of the required information is in a computer database, it takes an analyst several days to gather the information and reply to the client. Since information can change daily, an evaluation cannot be stored and reused for the next client. Expert systems materially alter the cost aspects of analysis and reduce service times several fold by updating and storing evaluations any time information changes. When a client calls, a current evaluation is always available for printing or electronic transfer.

Offensive Competitive Weapon

A common thread in the above applications is that they can be used as an offensive competitive weapon. Typically computer systems have been used defensively to hold down costs or as the only way to provide services and products competitively. By providing new revenue opportunities such as new or improved services, by finding ways to increase margins through improved decisions, by proactively controlling costs or stopping fraud, expert systems can be a powerful competitive weapon.

One company using an expert system to help deliver its product described the system as its "unfair competitive advantage." In late 1987 and early 1988 this point started to take hold, and a few companies found themselves in a clearly defensive position. These companies who had decided against expert system development were forced to reverse their position and are now playing catch up.

Focus

The next step in looking for potential applications is to focus on the leverage points within the organization that will provide the highest payback.

Time Constrained

Most production tasks are time constrained because the employee does not have the luxury of spending as much time as desired on each case. The time spent on the average case is set by management as the best compromise between quality and productivity. If quality is the dominant concern, productivity suffers and vice versa. Other applications, such as stock trading, are purely time constrained, and are not governed by either productivity or quality. Stock trading is an extreme example of a time constrained task since an enormous amount of information must be assimilated, sifted, and prioritized, and a decision rendered in minutes or seconds.

Regardless of whether the application is constrained by time, quality, or productivity, the central problems are information overload and lack of reasoning time. In many applications, such as stock trading, credit approval, underwriting, or order entry, expert systems can complete the decision process (information filtering, identification of relevant facts, problem organization, reasoning, and conclusion) faster and more thoroughly than the human mind. Time constrained applications normally use expert systems to collect and organize all information, shield the user from irrelevant information, and succinctly present the gist of the situation to the user with a recommendation.

Effectively, the expert system is being used as an investigative assistant whose purpose is to present a final recommendation contained on a one- or two-screen "executive summary." Properly used, expert systems improve quality while shortening the decision time, and are not likely to be influenced by emotion, pressure, or other distractions.

Volume Overload

Today there are hundreds of computer systems that handle thousands of transactions daily with only cursory checking because review by a qualified employee would be too time consuming and costly. Credit card purchase approval, bank teller transactions, benefit or claim payment approval, and group insurance underwriting are a few examples. The nature of the business requires the companies handling these transactions to accept the risk of fraud, which can be costly. In all of the above areas semi-autonomous expert systems are in use today that insert a qualified electronic employee in the process to stop fraud before it occurs.

For example, a Texas bank had a group of several auditors responsible for reviewing bank card transactions to identify cases of fraudulent use. Once they had confirmed fraud, the auditors would take whatever legal action was required to attempt recovery. The process was slow, not very effective, and worst of all, after-the-fact. The same bank has implemented an expert system that does all of the detective work in real time before-the-fact and can approve, disapprove, or defer approval on new transactions. The application uses confidence levels based on accumulated evidence, and depending on the confidence level, the system takes the appropriate action or immediately refers the case to an auditor for action.

Training

Some office procedures are straightforward and experience, knowledge, or decision times bear little relationship to job performance once a training program has been completed. In these situations, companies are using expert systems as training tools for new personnel. These allow new employees to begin contributing the first day on the job. The new employee does useful work under the guidance and control of an expert system. The new employee's productivity is far less than the norm; nevertheless productive work is being accomplished. This approach saves formal training, management, and supervision time.

Knowledge

Expert systems can be utilized to distribute and/or concentrate knowledge. Almost every multi-user application is an example of knowledge distribution; however, many applications are also examples of knowledge concentration. Knowledge concentration occurs when the system is built using multiple specialists or knowledge on broad and diverse subjects that most users would not have at their fingertips. The electric motor catalog selection application is an example of both knowledge concentration and distribution. Knowledge concentration creates a level of "expertise" that would normally be unattainable organizationally unless several individuals could be consulted on each and every case.

Expert systems can also be used to create an "expert" for new products or services. Typically, a new product or service requires a learning curve for field sales and service personnel, but initially no one in the organization has experience with the product. In these cases, central engineering, sales, and marketing personnel can be pooled to create an expert system for field personnel. This type of application could be built on the knowledge of the engineering staff to help repairmen diagnose and repair malfunctions in a new computer, machine, or other product. At the risk of belaboring an example, the electric motor catalog selection application represents another example where technical specifications and capabilities of a new motor are added to the system and combined with the sales savvy.

Manual Delivery

Tasks that depend on the use of policy, regulation, and procedure manuals are ideal expert system applications. Because knowledge is information in context, expert systems can be utilized to computerize manuals and deliver them to users in context with judgment and advice. One firm uses an expert system to monitor construction and maintenance practices to ensure that all applicable regulations and codes are followed. The potential range of government applications is enormous in screening eligibility for various programs such as welfare and medicaid. In addition to screening, systems could also identify the level of eligibility and ensure policy and regulations are interpreted consistently. The same is true for any corporate manual or policy.

Using expert systems for manual delivery eliminates the need for a great deal of employee research and boosts productivity. Manual delivery systems are also an ideal first application, since most, if not all, knowledge acquisition is complete – it is already written down in the form of a manual.

4

Benefits

Knowledge Dynamics

Being scarce commodities, knowledge and expertise cannot always be made available whenever and wherever needed. The significance of knowledge capture for business is that it permits knowledge and expertise to be accumulated, retained, and distributed to those parts of the organization where they can do the most good.

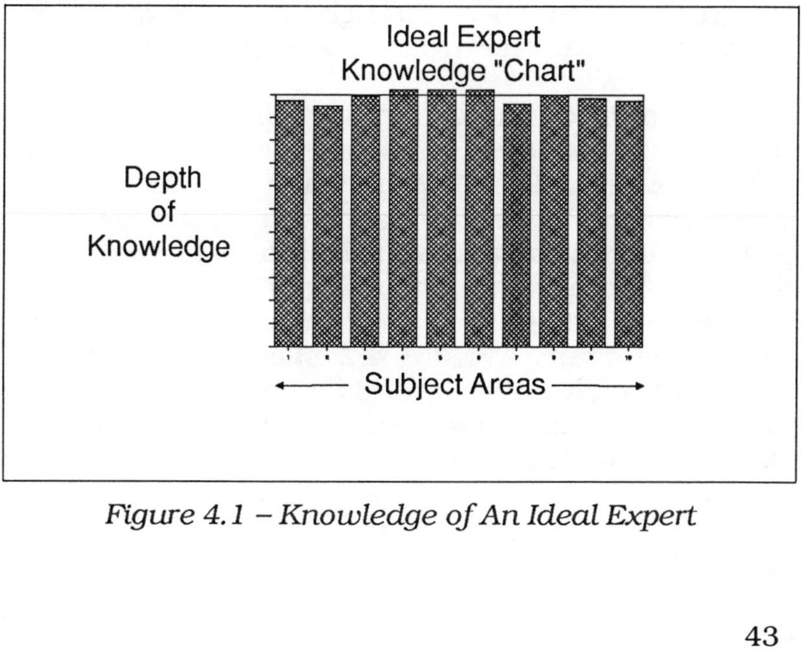

Figure 4.1 – Knowledge of An Ideal Expert

Of the three foundation benefits – new applications, alternative approaches, and knowledge capture – knowledge capture is the capstone. Books are a form of static knowledge, but expert systems are a form of kinetic knowledge that can be focused on analysis and problem resolution.

Expertise is knowledge in action, and it takes on many forms. In some applications, expertise requires little reasoning ability, but does require a command of the facts. When facts are nonexistent, incomplete, fragmented, or uncertain, expertise depends on reasoning and judgmental skills. Often, expertise is the combination of the two that spans multiple subject or specialty areas.

Individually, expertise can be acquired through experience, or it can be simulated by pooling the experience of multiple specialists. Knowledge engineering allows us to acquire expertise from the "teachings" of an expert, through time and experience, or by pooling the knowledge of several individuals.

The knowledge needed by an individual or system before he/it achieves competent performance levels can be conceptually represented by a bar chart like the one shown in Figure 4.1. Each bar represents a subject or specialty area, and the length of the bar represents the depth of knowledge. Experts are scarce, and rarely will any two individuals have the same knowledge chart. Figure 4.2 shows four different knowledge charts: two from different individuals and two representing additional knowledge acquired during two separate time periods.

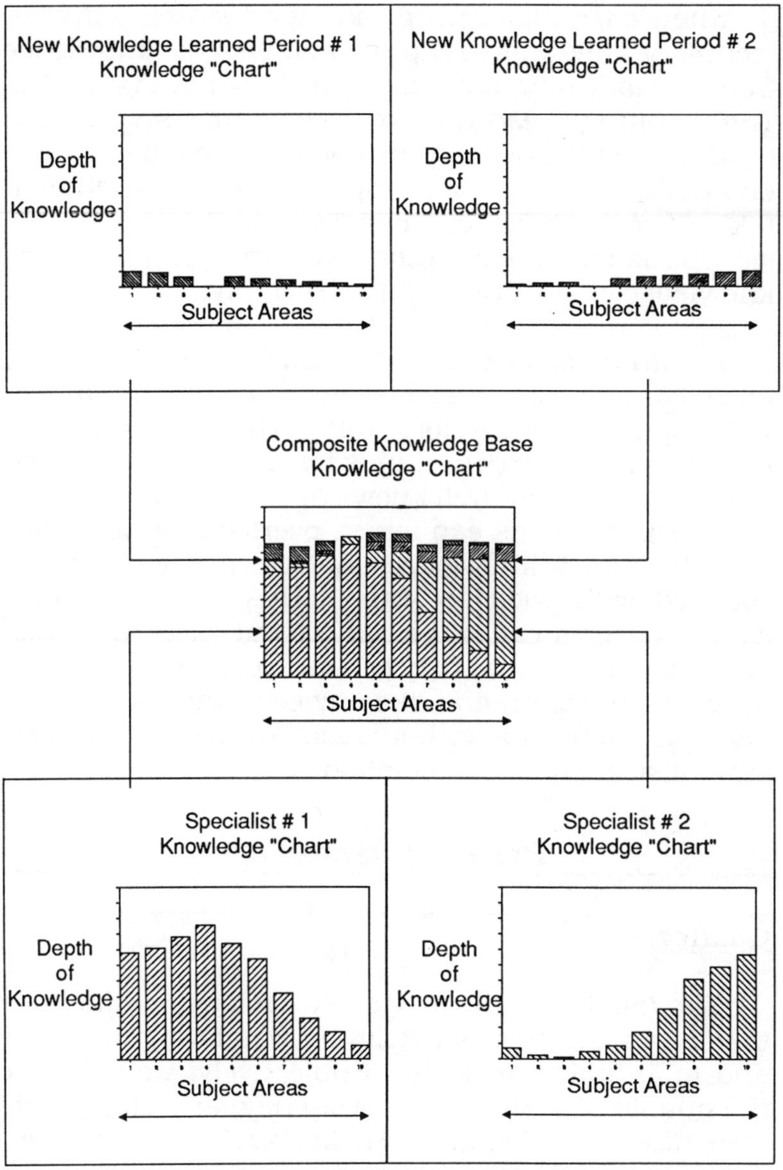

Figure 4.2 – Knowledge Concentration

Knowledge engineering and expert system software techniques allow us to capture and pool the knowledge from the four different charts as shown in Figure 4.2. The resulting breadth of knowledge may still be less than the optimum expert, but the usable pooled knowledge exceeds the competent level. Whether it takes three months, or three years, to become a subject specialist, an expert, or just competent, the same knowledge engineering principles apply.

Because of the breadth and accessibility of knowledge, expert systems enjoy a substantial advantage over the average user. The accessibility of knowledge is a particular plus for expert systems, and is a measure of how well knowledge is remembered and retrieved. Humans can forget, overlook, or be uncertain about their knowledge – frailties not normally associated with good software. This does not imply expert systems can out-smart or out-think the user, but it does imply that they can out-remember and out-thorough the user, and like any computer system are immune from fatigue, boredom, tunnel-vision, pressure, distractions, and emotion.

Primary Benefits

Quality

The quality of the analysis, decisions, and actions taken by a company's employees has both qualitative and quantitative aspects. Subjectively, we measure the quality of performance every day, and can clearly recognize one individual as being better than another. Experience indicates expert systems can perform as well as some of the better employees, and when multiple specialists are used, the systems can outperform most individuals.

Most of the discussions about the quality improvement provided by expert systems focus on technical knowledge, but in business applications policy knowledge can be equally important. Since companies want employees to use specific information, approaches, interpretations, and guidelines, clerical as well as professional decisions are governed to some extent by company policy and procedure. Employees can be trained, tested, and trusted, but management can never be certain that employees are adhering to company policy unless every decision is reviewed. Incorrect or less than optimum decisions are seldom deliberate; they are normally an honest mistake caused by a lack of communication, time, training, or experience. Being the creation and property of management, knowledge bases can contain policy knowledge as well as technical task-specific knowledge.

The most experienced and competent employees are usually supervisors and managers not directly involved in the task-level decisions where their experience would be extremely valuable. Mentor and assistant applications that capture the expertise of these employees can provide review and recommendation assistance to employees on each case they handle. Expert systems provide the best of both worlds – the experience of the supervisors can be concentrated and provided to all employees electronically – and the supervisors are still free to leverage their personal knowledge over wider areas of responsibility. The resulting effect is that each situation is reviewed twice: once by the employee, and once by the electronic clone of the supervisor. In production or highly critical applications, the second opinion provided by the system can produce substantial savings in error reduction, and/or increase profit through improved customer satisfaction or improved selection of the most optimum solution. Nonproduction, ad hoc applications, where a user's knowledge and problem structuring skills may not be fresh and up-to-date, can also benefit from expert systems which provide guidance and structure assistance to users.

Control

Expert systems can be used to improve control over many aspects of operations. One side of control is the ability to monitor and audit operations to identify variations from standard. Production or integrated systems equipped with reporting capability add a new and important dimension to management reporting. Conventional systems can report what happened, but cannot make judgments about the desirability of what transpired. Expert systems, in contrast, have knowledge of both aspects and can report on both.

The other side of control is closely related to the quality issue. Auditing checks the effectiveness of an entire process including quality control. Typically, quality control checks for errors after the fact. Expert systems integrates quality control into the process by providing checks and guidance during production.

Expert systems do not think for the user, but guide him to the right decision. Experience with production systems shows users quickly recognize this, and view the system not as an adversary, but as part of the team.

Consistency

Consistency has its roots in quality and control. Externally, part of a company's image may depend on the consistency of service levels and application of policy. Internally, consistency is important to assure fairness, control costs, and improve operations. If computer systems are anything, they are relentlessly consistent, and expert systems are no different.

Secondary Benefits

The benefit structure of expert systems is recursive, and the primary benefits create a ripple effect that gives rise to secondary benefits. Often, the value of the secondary benefits may be greater than the primary. All of the secondary benefits have intrinsic value, but by providing more time to handle difficult cases, by providing ways to improve, and by leveraging a company's professional these benefits also provide the means to improve quality even further.

Improvement

Some companies track decisions made by their professional staffs to monitor the quality of the decisions. For these companies, auditing results and establishing cause-and-effect relationships can be formidable tasks, because human decisions introduce the variables of uniform quality, management control, and consistency into the equation. Properly designed, an expert system knows what happened and if the decision was suspect. With this information it can provide substantial auditing assistance and the management information needed to analyze cause-and-effect relationships.

Because expert systems can model the human decision process using management-supplied information, they can also be used as proactive modeling tools. In a complex marketplace, management may wish to change decision guidelines to increase revenue, decrease risk, or achieve some other goal. Without a sophisticated modeling tool, management can only make an educated guess at the needed policy changes. With an expert system, the new policy can be tested against a sample set of cases. Cause-and-effect relationships become clearer, and management can be assured policy changes will achieve the desired result.

One subtle way expert systems help companies improve is through the knowledge engineering process. The knowledge engineering process demands that the organization examine, understand, and agree with the complex reasoning process of its experts. This process often leads to pleasant as well as unpleasant surprises, but once the process is laid out and understood it can be improved. Characteristically the first time a company (or an expert) fully understands its policies, guidelines, and decision criteria is after completing an expert system.

Productivity

Productivity is often cited as a primary benefit, but productivity increases are generally a secondary result of a well-designed application. The key elements behind productivity increases were discussed earlier. Semi-autonomous systems can improve productivity by screening incoming work and taking autonomous action on intermediate decisions, and cases can be prescreened, analyzed, and presented to the user in summary form to save the employee time.

Professional Leveraging

Expert systems are often viewed as a way to give the skilled professional back his job. Organizations usually have one or more employees who are constantly barraged with questions and problems from other employees. By helping employees answer the routine questions and solve routine problems, expert systems can allow the professional to use his skill and knowledge on other, more demanding tasks.

This type of leveraging also has a ripple effect. In one example, a company built an expert system to diagnose computer hardware and software problems for a large number of users that were scattered over the entire United States. Before the system was put in place, only one technical individual had the breadth of experience needed to accurately diagnose user problems, and he had to spend most of his day on the phone as a troubleshooter rather than do his real job. When the expert system was put into operation the number of requests for help went up dramatically and then tailed off to a level much lower than the pre-system level. The number of service requests was only an indication of what happened. The rise in demand occurred because the system was more accessible and more problems were being solved in a shorter time. The decline in demand was the result of the learning experience the system provided, and after a while users were able to solve most problems without help.

Professional leveraging also occurs at the system user level as a result of productivity increases. Because standard cases can be handled quicker, and difficult cases can be preanalyzed, users can have more time to work on difficult cases. If all of the productivity gains were to be reapplied to the difficult and challenging cases, there would be no change in productivity, but the effectiveness of the professional staff would increase.

Section II

Perspectives

5

Roots

Every book on expert systems has an obligatory chapter on the history of artificial intelligence. However, the mere reporting of historic events only establishes a framework. A historian has the luxury of 20/20 hindsight and the freedom to choose the perspective from which to interpret history. Hindsight allows us to understand the nature, problems, failures, successes, and potential of the technology. The perspective chosen stems from the needs of commercial applications. The purpose here is to gain an understanding of the AI community as well as the technology and industry it created.

Cognitive Psychology

Artificial intelligence has it roots in cognitive psychology, not computer science. Before World War II, scientists had begun to explore the inner workings of the human mind. Scientists were studying learning, knowledge, and cognitive processes.

Shortly after World War II, the computer era began. Scientists, eager to test their cognitive psychology theories, began using computers as a research tool. Scientists could easily convert theories explaining various aspects of human cognition into computer models. Computers proved to be valuable research tools for testing and demonstration. Thus, in the marriage of computers and cognitive psychology, artificial intelligence was conceived. In the ten years following World War II, the research led to some very important questions, and scientists began to grapple with definitions of both human and machine intelligence.

The Formative Years

During the next five years, from 1955 to 1960, AI began to take shape. LISP, a development of the era, would become the predominant language for AI programming. Researchers gave their new technology a name at the 1956 Dartmouth conference on machine intelligence by coining the term *artificial intelligence.*

Scientists believed they could easily explain, model, and implement human cognition using electronic computers. Fueled by imagination, excitement grew. The potential ramifications were profound. Intelligent machines based on the new "electronic brains" could alter the course of civilization.

The enthusiasm carried the research community through the sixties. Having underestimated the problem, the research community made seemingly outlandish claims. Soon computers would be able to learn, reason independently, and might even be capable of original thought. Some even speculated computers would soon outperform the human mind.

The scientists did make progress, but they failed to produce anything close to their goals or promises. The sixties, characterized by unrealistic goals, produced an overabundance of promises but no deliverable capability. Disappointment quenched the fire of enthusiasm and AI fell into disfavor. Discredited and labeled as dreamers, AI believers became embattled outcasts.

In retrospect, the research was sound but its goal was too general and broad. The goal was to find THE singular set of general models capable of explaining intelligence. Again in retrospect, the research was bound to be extremely complex because the problem was one of great depth and breadth. If successful, the research would have been the ultimate in "Big Bang" development, vaulting technology from the primitive IBM 1401 computer to HAL (the computer in the movie *2001*) in one giant step.

Significant in this period was the establishment of research centers at Stanford, Dartmouth, Carnegie-Mellon (CMU), and the Massachusetts Institute of Technology (MIT). During the next decade, these centers would play a major role in shaping the technology as we know it today.

Regrouping

Focus

The decade of the seventies was a regrouping period. The AI community examined their goals and made them more realistic, paring both the depth and the breadth of the research. The search turned from general cognitive models to narrowly defined problem solving.

Backing away from the broad goals of the sixties forced some limitations. Scientists rightly contended the definition of intelligence must include common sense, learning, and independent as well as creative thought. The tighter focus recognized intelligence was not the prerequisite for useful application, and attention turned to knowledge storage and decision-making ability within a limited scope. This was, and still is, a pragmatic and acceptable limitation.

During the decade, research continued at the academic research centers but research also began at Xerox PARC (Palo Alto Research Center) and at Digital Equipment Corporation. Xerox, one of the early leaders, made great progress producing many new techniques and approaches. Some of these – the mouse, windowing, graphics, and icons – later found their way to Apple Computer. The origin of these techniques and AI's heavy reliance on them has led to incorrect beliefs that they are an inseparable part of AI programs.

The Challenges

To move the technology ahead, researchers needed to overcome both software and hardware hurdles. Conventional programming languages were too cumbersome and confining for AI development. Since AI applications are nonprocedural and deal with symbols rather than data, the researchers needed to develop new nonprocedural and symbolic computer languages. In addition, the complexity of AI programming requires a flexible, powerful and efficient development environment for the programmer to use. The cornerstone of the new programmer development environments was a highly interactive and facile programmer interface that used mice, icons, and graphics to communicate complex symbolic information to the programmer.

Computer power was limited and AI research was constantly pushing the upper limits of hardware capability. Existing computer architectures supported numerical and procedural processing; however, the cognitive models under development were nonnumeric and nonprocedural. To implement these models the researchers believed powerful new computers with radically different architectures were required. Even with these new powerful tools, researchers felt AI applications were so computer intensive that multi-user machines were unworkable.

LISP, which had become the standard computer language for AI development, was seen as the key ingredient in the solution to both the hardware and software problems. LISP provided the needed software capabilities but it did not run efficiently on standard computers. To solve the hardware problem LISP computers were introduced. These computers were designed for symbolic computing and were specifically optimized for running LISP programs.

The technology and the tools under development confined researchers to the application box shown in Figure 5.1. At this juncture, 99% of the problem was developing the hardware and software technology capable of handling symbolic and nonprocedural problems. Thus integration with conventional hardware and software was correctly ignored since it was outside of the problem scope.

Shaping the Technology

With the hardware and software challenges understood and the solutions generally agreed upon, the researchers began to develop expert system applications. The basic R & D mode was prototyping because it was ideally suited to the nature of AI research. Prototyping, discounted by some as a crude trial-and-error approach, is an ideal development method for ill-defined and ill-understood problems. The approach was to

Figure 5.1 – Early Seventies Application Niche

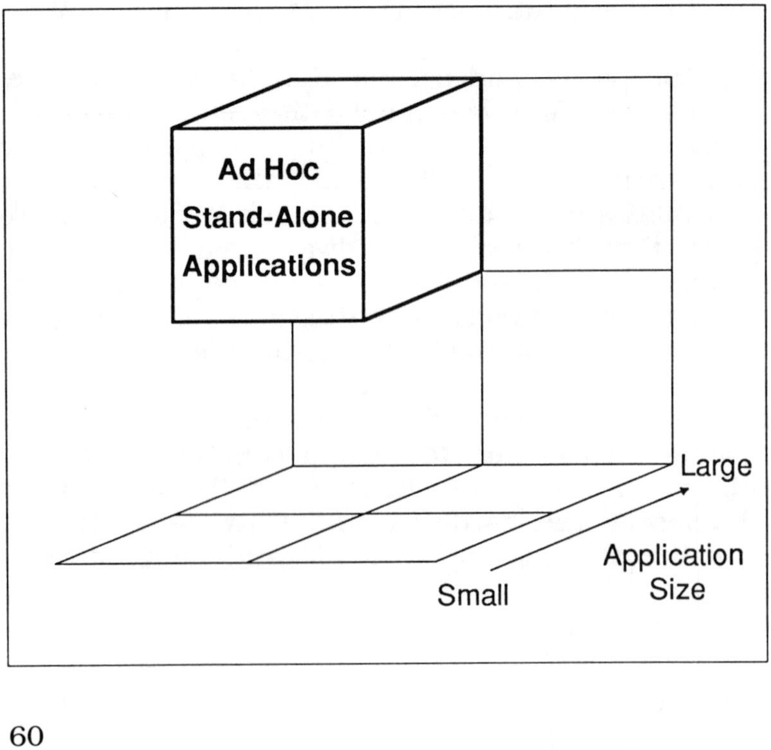

build, test, and evaluate. If improvements or error corrections were desirable or necessary, the software was changed and the cycle repeated until the desired results were obtained.

The requirements for AI development, i.e., a LISP-based, graphics-oriented prototyping environment, were singular in the computer industry. The research goal was to develop, test, and prove capability: delivery, user productivity, and integration with other computer systems were not yet major issues. The AI researchers had carved out a comfortable niche in the application cube, and to a certain extent, the immaturity of the technology confined them to this small niche.

Birth of an Industry

As the seventies came to an end, AI had matured to the point where some aspects were usable in a business environment. When unified, these aspects represented what we know today as expert systems.

In 1978, the development of the first production system for order assembly at Digital Equipment marked the birth of commercial expert systems. As expert systems left the lab, businessmen and scientists formed a number of new corporations. Venture capital gravitated to those companies whose founders, scientists, and employees had the strongest research pedigree. The following list shows some of the research centers and the companies they spawned.

Carnegie-Mellon University
- Carnegie Group - 1983
- PERQ - Production Technologies - 1983
- Artelligence - 1985

Massachusetts Institute of Technology
- LMI (LISP Machines Inc.) - 1980
- Symbolics - 1980
- Teknowledge - 1981
- Gold Hill - 1982
- Thinking Machines Corporation - 1983
- Palladian Software - 1984

Stanford University
- IntelliCorp - 1980
- Symantec - 1982
- Syntelligence - 1983

Yale
- Cognitive Systems - 1981
- Smart Systems Technology - 1981

Miscellaneous
- Dartmouth - AIC (Artificial Intelligence Corp.) - 1975
- Brigham Young - Automated Language Processing - 1980
- Berkeley - Franz Inc. - 1984

Marketing personnel believe the name of a company should say something about the enterprise. Assuming these new companies followed this advice, a reading of the names is revealing. These companies were technology brokers and their mission was to deliver the software and hardware tools needed to build end-user products. Since competition among vendors was based on the technical superiority of their respective products, more technology was good and the more sophisticated the technology the better.

The advent of the order assembly system at Digital expanded the application cube to production systems. In parallel with the early expert system industry formation, the personal computer was experiencing its early growth. Some expert system vendors developed down-sized and simplified development tools for the growing personal computer market. In a few short years, the application cube had grown to encompass small personal computer applications and production systems as shown in Figure 5.2. Integration was still a few years away.

Figure 5.2 – Expert System Applications – Early Eighties

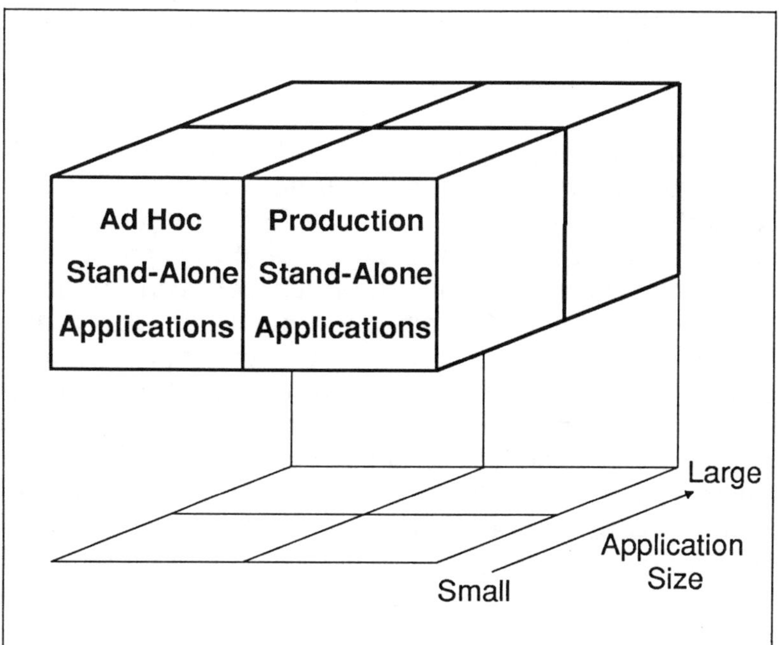

The Early Market

Large Applications

The market boomed while large research labs and the defense department consumed machines, software and technologists. The law of supply and demand was in full force so prices were high and cost justification was not a major factor in the purchase decisions.

The defense department and defense contractors made up the largest market for the new companies. In addition to unmanned weapon systems, complex battle management Command, Control and Communication systems were under investigation. The thrust was to research and develop military applications. System delivery was a totally separate issue. Once complete, the system would use special chips for weapon delivery.

Small Applications

In the small applications area, the software needed to develop expert systems on personal computers flooded the market. Many of these early products were limited by computer power and lacked the sophistication of the tools used for the larger technical applications. Dismissed as toys by vendors in the large application market, they were not taken seriously. Undaunted, some innovative companies purchased these tools as an inexpensive way to learn and in many cases produced valuable end-user systems. However, regardless of whether the application was large or small, most were stand-alone applications for use in a nonproduction environment.

The Early Industry

Responding to market needs, the expert system industry began to take shape. Hardware companies such as LMI and Symbolics sprung up to produce expensive but efficient LISP machines designed to support the needs of the prototyping environment. By definition, they were single-user machines designed for development and technical users. Computer integration capability was limited to connecting one LISP processor to another.

At the same time, software tool vendors emerged. Intellicorp, Inference, Teknowledge, and the Carnegie Group became so prominent they were nicknamed The Gang of Four. In keeping with military and technical market needs, their products were highly effective single-user tools.

Although successful in their chosen market, the expert system industry lacked breadth. In practical terms, the expert system community had by coincidence become a closed society. Virtually the only way to enter the society was through academic, military, or technical channels and the industry maintained close ties with the research community. Their market demanded little more than the original research had provided in the stand-alone application niche. Few of the original research tenants or assumptions were challenged and through repetition they were elevated to the status of dogma. The narrow application and technical focus would soon begin to change once the technical market reached saturation and market demographics began to shift.

Market Transition

In 1985, the expert system market was a technology-driven market, but two forces were at work that would effect a major market transition. The first of these was the saturation of the military and technical markets. Because of the high cost of expert system hardware and software, their purchases were often considered capital expenditures. In the early market, demand for these products was high and the number of vendors small. Once the initial needs of the market had been met, sales slumped and demand was dictated by normal maintenance and growth. The decline in demand was also exacerbated by the growing number of vendors which foretold of fierce price and product competition. To survive, the industry needed to cultivate additional markets that were more difficult and costly to reach.

The second force was the growing interest in commercial applications which would provide the needed new market. Some innovative commercial companies adopted the technology and began developing end-user applications. Expert system development was underway for applications such as insurance underwriting, loan application review, and medical claims processing.

As these user-oriented systems moved through development, the emphasis shifted. Applications under development were for delivery to dozens or perhaps thousands of users. For these applications, it was not economical to provide each user with specialized hardware and software. Instead, applications would have to run on conventional hardware and IBM had the largest installed base of computers, none of which were LISP processors. Commercial applications would use the technology differently than military or technical applications. The technology was sound and beneficial, but not fully usable unless productivity and integration issues were resolved.

The tools had been built to handle complex technical applications. The new office applications were simpler and required only a fraction of the power and flexibility of the available tools. The unneeded capability added overhead, consumed memory, and adversely affected computer response time. The development and run-time versions of the tools were so closely intertwined that total rewrites would be required to separate them. Until separated, production applications would suffer under the added overhead of the development environment. Office applications would have to run on traditional computers in a multiuser environment. From a commercial standpoint, the days of the dedicated LISP computer were over. A new set of requirements had emerged.

New Challenges

Products of a research environment, few vendors understood the commercial data processing environment. They would be sorely tested. The easiest of the new requirements to address was integration, but even that would be a formidable task due to the structure of the tools. Since the mid-seventies, computer power had grown rapidly and costs were falling at an equally amazing rate. This partially invalidated the assumptions of the seventies about specialized hardware. Thus the tools were translated from LISP to languages better suited for standard computers, and the first simple language interfaces were added. The application cube was again expanded but productivity and complete integration issues were still unaddressed.

Vendor Challenges

The technology was no longer driving the market, the market was beginning to drive the technology. The expert system vendors were on the horns of a dilemma. Because of their research heritage, the emerging market was different from what they had anticipated. Their products stood apart from most commercial data processing standards. Furthermore, the vendors had little expertise in mainstream data processing. They had made huge investments in their products and it would take both time and even more money to completely resolve the integration and productivity issues.

The vendors supplying expert system tools to the personal computer market faced the same challenges but to a lesser extent. Local area networks, micro-to-mainframe interfaces, and standardization on a few database and spreadsheet packages made the integration issues easier to resolve. In addition, the rapid growth in personal computer power and the relatively low capital investment required by PCs allowed vendors to continually improve the quality and sophistication of their products. The personal computer products were growing up and were no longer toys; they were becoming useful and sophisticated tools.

The Current State

The challenges facing the vendors are broader than depicted here. The industry is still young and small but the market is diverse containing many specialty areas. The needs of the military, manufacturing, engineering, aerospace, financial, and commercial market segments are all different. Each segment, with its own perspective and application of the technology, places different requirements on vendor-supplied tools. The market, being too small to support specialty vendors, is still generalized and the vendors are unable to be all things to all people. As the industry matures, it is reasonable to assume it will mirror the current computer industry with multiple specialty vendors.

Figure 5.3 – Expert System Applications – 1988

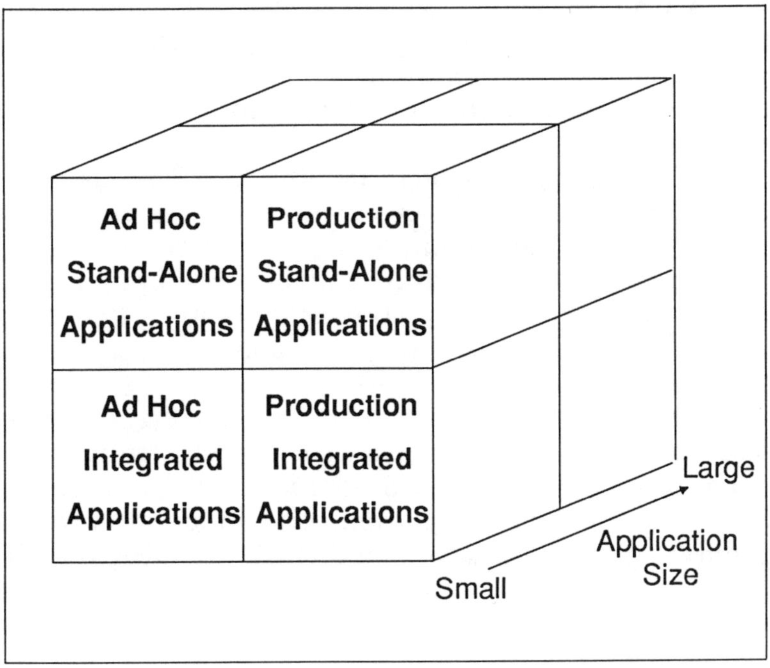

To date, the vendors have responded admirably but the market is still in a state of transition. Since 1987, vendors have been announcing and delivering numerous integration and productivity improvements in their products. Leading edge companies are quickly assimilating these improvements and integrated production systems are appearing that complete the application cube shown in Figure 5.3.

Most of the commercial application technical barriers have been removed. Much of the work that lies ahead for the vendors is refining and enhancing the usability of their tools.

Summary

As expert system technology took its first steps toward commercialization in the early eighties, the expert system's community, including vendors, was a closed society. Prior to commercialization, all research was concentrated on developing the ability to build and demonstrate expert system technology. The applications developed in the seventies were large technical applications that required neither high end-user productivity, nor integration with other computer systems. The objective was to build capability rather than deliver usable commercial applications.

The expert systems market in the early eighties was dominated by the Pentagon and high-end technical applications. This market did not require the vendors to alter the research orientation of the tools they were producing. Early market success elevated the beliefs of the research community to the status of dogma that could be applied universally to all expert system applications.

About 1985, market forces shifted the emphasis from capability to deliverability. In this market shift, production and integrated applications became as important as the ad hoc and stand-alone applications of earlier years. The market shift forced the vendors to reexamine many of their assumptions and change the shape and orientation of their products.

6

The Tracks of Change

The future of AI is still uncertain. Pessimists believe it will die a quiet and perhaps ignoble death. They claim it died in the sixties and its current resurrection will not alter the inevitable outcome. Others take a long view and believe it has its own manifest destiny and will replace data processing as we know it today. Comment on these predictions is not possible without placing them in context. If the context includes all of AI, the long view of AI governs. If the context includes only expert systems, both camps are probably half right, but in ways they might not expect.

From a business perspective, expert systems are not a total solution because they cannot solve the full spectrum of business problems. Since they are only effective in specific applications, they cannot replace data processing as we know it today. They will, however, have a significant impact on the evolution of data processing.

Stand-alone expert systems can be viewed as distinct self-contained solutions; however, expert systems integrated into the corporate data processing environment represent an augmentation technology. As such, the technology is not self-contained but it can assist and extend the capabilities of conventional software. As an augmentation technology, it will be slowly assimilated into the traditional data processing environment. As the assimilation continues, it will be accepted as the norm, rather than AI. The assimilation may appear to be the slow death predicted, but instead it is a maturing process.

We can't predict where the technology is headed. Perhaps over the next several years trends will develop pointing the way. From today's perspective, we lack the knowledge and experience to make concrete predictions. However, historical trends provide insights that help us understand the present as well as what the future might bring.

Technology Evolution

Historically, the application of a new technology evolves through a four-phase process.

- Imitation. The technology is defined relative to existing technology. Its application is defined by and limited to existing business procedures and practices.

- Investigation. The technology is still defined relative to existing technology. Its application is limited to improving current business procedures and practices.

- Experimentation. The technology begins to define itself. Its application modifies current business procedures and practices.

- Innovation. The technology is defined in its own terms. Its application completely alters and redefines business procedures and practices.

The four phases represent a natural evolution that occurs simultaneously in the business and vendor communities. A growth process, it reflects an increased level of understanding, confidence, and maturity. In the first phase, the technology is in search of a problem to solve. In the last, the problems search out the technology. All technologies evolve through these phases. Current computer technology is still evolving, but it provides an example of the evolutionary process.

Imitation

As a technology emerges from the laboratory, it faces its first and most important hurdle. Scientists comprehend the technology, but don't fully appreciate its business uses. Businessmen understand business applications, but can't quite fathom the technology.

Each lacking the experience of the other, the scientist and the businessman form an alliance. With his new bag of tools, the scientist tours the office looking for something to fix or improve. The businessman wants to help but he must be cautious due to society's natural tendency to resist change. Eventually the businessman selects a safe, comfortable, and familiar application easily understood and justified. The application is an existing practice or procedure and the technology is carefully molded to fit within organizational norms. Old practices and procedures are carefully preserved and the new technology is simply used to replicate what was there before. The only thing new is the technology – the result is imitation.

The early use of electronic computers is a good example of imitation. When computers were first introduced, mechanical tab card operations were referred to as data processing. Businesses used the new computers to speed up the older tab card systems. The result was a new type of tab card system; the same in every way, except now electronic computers were used. To distinguish the new from the old, terminology was changed from data processing to *electronic* data processing.

At introduction, automobiles exhibited a classic form of imitation. They weren't even called automobiles – they were horseless carriages. They even looked like carriages with the only concessions made being a place for the engine, a throttle, and a steering tiller to replace the horse's reins. Even the steering tiller was an imitation of an existing technology, the boat rudder.

In this first phase, users are skeptical and lack confidence. For example, at the dawn of the computer age, it was accepted that no computer could be trusted to calculate premiums or account balances. Such sensitive things had to be done by human beings.

During the imitation phase, the first applications are marginal at best. Typically, the tools are crude, immature, and lack many needed capabilities. Because the technology is molded to the environment, only a small fraction of the potential benefits are realized and even they are misunderstood.

Existing business practices and cost justification structures are shaped by experiences with existing technology. They form a yardstick by which all applications are measured. Unfortunately, as a new technology emerges, it is measured with yesterday's yardstick. Often this is an apples to oranges comparison.

The yardstick problem is a symptom of the experience-expectation loop. Experiences form the basis for establishing expectations including expected uses and benefits. Experience creates tangible mental reference points and the more experience we have, the closer expectations mirror reality. As expectations become more realistic, the quality of the experiences improve and the experiential reference points become more tangible.

With a new technology, we fall back on prior experiences. Experiences built on old technology are only partly applicable to the new. As a result, expectations are too high, too low, wrong, or misdirected.

Investigation

In the second phase, confidence begins to build based on past adequate performance. As demand increases, vendor competition becomes important. The technology matures, and becomes cheaper and easier to use. Building on past experience, businesses begin to see the technology as a way to improve on old procedures. The old procedures stay in place but are enhanced through newly discovered shortcuts.

Continuing the computer analogy, the investigative phase is exemplified by early on-line applications. These applications provided little processing capability and were limited to data capture and editing. In the old procedure, clerks completed coding sheets, submitted them to keypunch, and waited for the return of batch edit reports. Errors were corrected through a recoding and resubmission process.

The early on-line applications changed neither the goal nor the fundamental process except that the latter was now on-line. Yet, the technology was beginning to provide real payback. By replacing the paper coding form with an electronic one, substantial shortcuts were found. The technology increased productivity, reduced time delays, and eliminated the entire keypunch department.

Experimentation

Until the beginning of the experimentation phase, a technology is defined in relation to experiences with older technologies. Definitions or explanations begin with phrases similar to: "It is like . . . ." By the time the experimentation phase is reached, this practice ceases.

Understanding the subtle nuances of a foreign language provides insights into other cultures. Many of the nuances may be unexplainable in the absence of the culture and its native tongue. The same is true of technology. The technology can now be defined in its own terms and in its own language because businesses now understand it and have ample experience. This is a subtle but important step forward because rather than just knowing about the technology, businesses now understand it.

This allows a technology to develop its own identity unrestrained by past convention. As a technology matures, social and technical barriers dissolve. With a newfound appreciation, businessmen no longer accept the "but we have never done it that way" arguments. Serious experimentation begins unfettered by past practices.

Again, computers provide a good example. As computer capability evolved, batch programs began to disappear. On-line batch data collection programs were transformed into new programs capable of sophisticated update and retrieval processing. The term electronic data processing was no longer in vogue – it had been replaced by information processing.

Organizationally, departmental boundaries still existed. Each department still had its own system. Transaction routing slips were still used for multi-department transactions, but the technology was providing greater benefits and a faster return on investment.

Innovation

By the time the innovation stage is reached, the technology's use does not appear to be innovative. Instead the new uses appear to be the natural extension of a useful technology. However, the new applications under development would be considered revolutionary by standards prevalent in the imitation phase.

In the computer evolution example, unit records storing data were replaced by small, highly organized data base records. The emphasis shifted from data to information and from processing to integration. Organizations were no longer shaping the technology to fit predefined molds. Instead, organizational structures changed as organizations adapted to the new technology to take full advantage of its potential.

This step was not made without organizational pain. Auditors accustomed to batch auditing practices had to develop new procedures. Managers also had to become accustomed to new procedures since now almost anyone in the organization could affect the computer system, not just specific departments. Inventory numbers could be impacted by transactions entered by marketing, production, shipping, or sales. Accounting systems were automatically updated by non-accountants in almost every department.

The transformation of the computer from electronic data processing to information management is a good example of evolution. At the dawn of the computer era, IBM predicted the total computer market would be less than a few dozen. This may be the worst marketing projection in history, but it was based on sound conventional wisdom and a lot of experience. Predictably, neither correctly told them what to expect.

Expert systems are now somewhere between the imitation and investigation phases. Things are moving slower than some would expect because of the lack of dialogue and the experience-expectation problem. The expectation problem is magnified with expert systems because of subtle but important differences from conventional software. Because of the subtleties, more education is necessary and it will take longer for the technology to be defined in its own terms. However, if history is any predictor, the way we will be using expert systems in the year 2000 will not resemble current usage.

Technology Diffusion

Figure 6.1 shows a technology diffusion curve depicting the level of expectation for a technology over time. At introduction, there is a general excitement. As it emerges from the laboratory, the champions and marketing gurus oversell and overcommit. Enthusiasm builds until the early adopters begin to report disappointing results. The results are disappointing from two standpoints. First, the benefits are far short of those promised and, second, the early imitative applications do not fully exploit the technology.

Early disappointment fuels a continuing devaluation until the technology is substantially undervalued. However, those who continue investigation and experimentation soon begin to report success. Soon, stock in the technology begins to rise until expectations meet the capability.

AI has followed a curve similar to that shown in Figure 6.2. Having gone through one complete cycle, it is now apparently in its second. The first cycle of enthusiasm began in the sixties. Intent on replicating human thought, scientists overpromised and underdelivered. Enthusiasm quickly gave way to a complete dismissal. With a narrower focus, research in the seventies bore fruit and interest increased. As AI left the lab about 1980, it was again oversold.

Figure 6.1 – Technology Diffusion Cycle

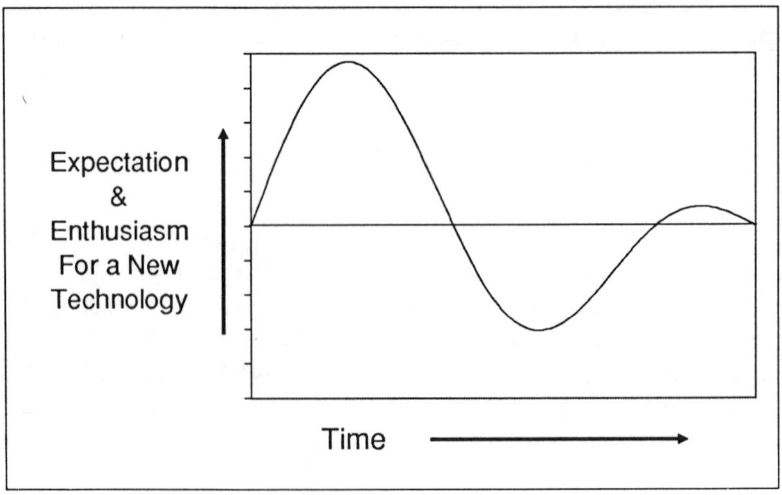

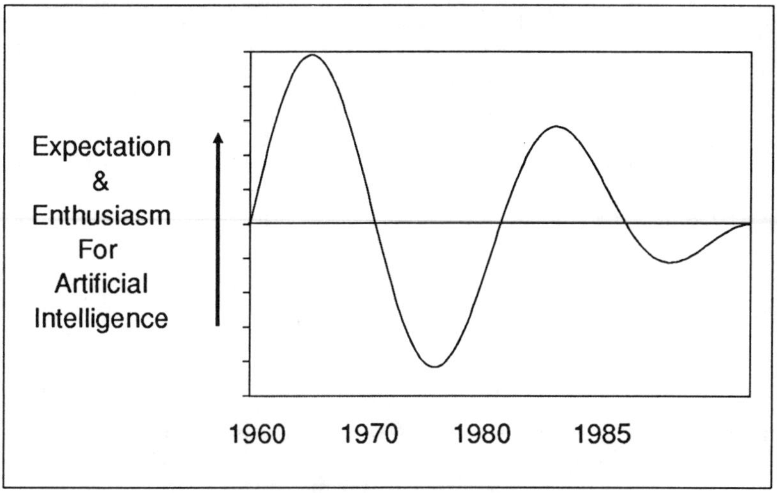

Figure 6.2 – Artificial Intelligence Diffusion Cycle

A technology may go through several cycles, but only one major cycle with wide swings in expectation is the norm. Artificial intelligence has apparently gone through two cycles as shown in Figure 6.2. More specifically, Figure 6.2 shows the diffusion cycle of two distinct technologies superimposed on each other. The composite diffusion cycle shown in Figure 6.3 is a better representation. The AI technology of the sixties never made it out of the lab. In the seventies, the technology was radically changed in scope and focus. Whether this was the death of sixties technology or its transformation is a matter of semantics. Even with the transformation, AI in its broadest sense is still in the lab. The second cycle belongs to expert systems, not AI.

Expert system specifics should not be confused with the generalities of AI. What is true of the whole is not necessarily true of each of the parts. Albeit a by-

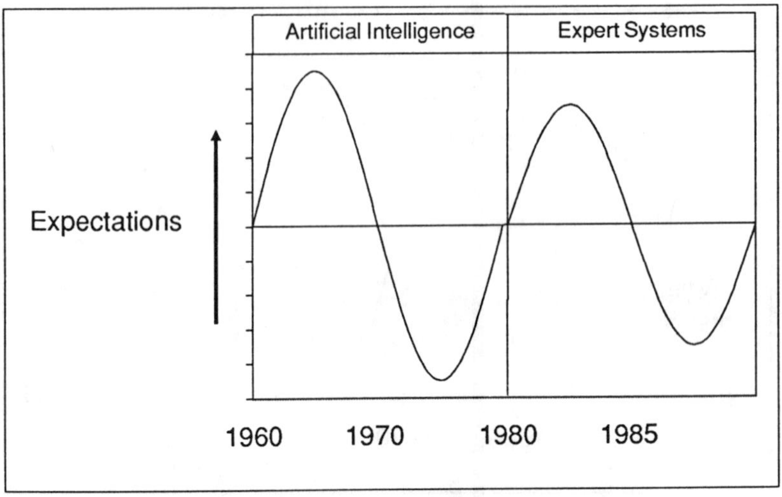

Figure 6.3 – Composite Diffusion Cycle

product of AI, expert systems should be viewed as a distinct technology. What we have seen since 1980 is a diffusion cycle for expert systems.

Technological Discontinuities

Over time, the use of a specific technology follows the traditional diminishing return curve shown in Figure 6.4. Investments yield positive benefits up to a point. Every technology has an upper limit defined by the point of diminishing returns.

The general growth of technology does not follow a single, continuous, and orderly diminishing return curve. New technologies appear that create technological discontinuities. The new technology with the same or similar application replaces or augments the older one. In doing so, the new technology superimposes its own cost/benefit characteristics on top of the older

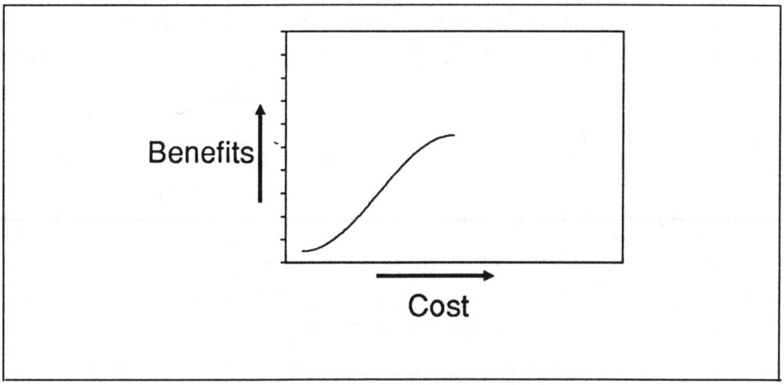

Figure 6.4 – Diminishing Return

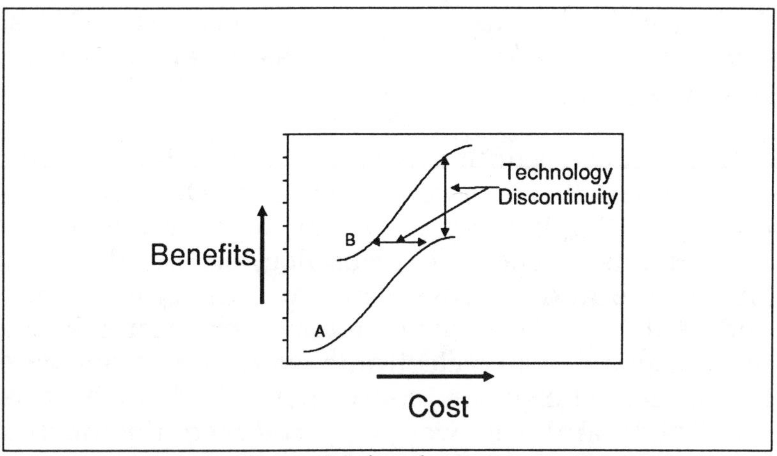

Figure 6.5 – Technology Discontinuity

curve. The result is the situation shown in Figure 6.5. The newer technology (curve B) creates a two dimensional discontinuity. The capability and benefits of the new technology are greater than the old technology as shown by the vertical separation of the two curves. The second dimension is the decrease in cost for equivalent benefit as shown by the horizontal separation of the two curves. Taken individually or together, the discontinuities alter the cost/benefit equation.

Technological discontinuities can be parallel, replacement, or augmenting. Parallel technologies open up new applications that change the way we work and partially replace the older technology. Replacement technologies completely displace the older technology. Augmentation occurs when a new technology is complementary and can be combined with older ones to substantially extend the capability of both. At a detail level, a new technology can exhibit all three of these characteristics depending on the circumstances. When this occurs, as is the case with expert systems, it is best to view the technology as an augmentation technology.

A parallel discontinuity can be seen in the histories of the typewriter and word processor. Over the years the typewriter has gone through many refinements. Investments in typewriter technology produced electric typewriters and improved size, weight, type quality, and usability. These investments were cost effective up to a point. Once electronic word processors were introduced, the upper limit of potential benefits was redefined, and the way we produced documents changed. Documents could be quickly entered, changed, stored, distributed, and printed. Under competitive pressure, typewriter manufacturers stretched their technology by adding automatic correction, memory, and other features. Still the typewriter could not compete with the word processor in certain areas. New typewriter features provided marginal benefits and only drove up the cost. The fact remained that typewriters couldn't compete with word processors for many applications and vice versa.

Even though there is still a place for the typewriter, new technologies can create virtually a complete replacement. Xerography replaced carbon paper. Personal computers replaced word processors. Cold type replaced hot lead type.

Database and expert systems both represent augmentation technologies. By themselves they are of little value, until combined with other conventional data processing technologies. Taken together each magnifies the capability of the other and extends the upper benefit limits.

The significance of this discontinuity to management is the way organizations react to it. Typically, companies have large investments in old technologies so new technologies are resisted to preserve these past investments. Companies try to extend the life of older technologies by adding new features and capabilities typically beyond the point of diminishing returns. These companies, try as they may, will not be able to halt the progress of technology. What is inevitable is inevitable.

To remain competitive, companies often must scrap older technologies. The prominence of IBM is testimony to this. IBM scrapped huge investments in tab card technology in favor of the electronic computer. Later IBM chose to kill its most profitable operation, the computer card division, by adopting strategies leading to magnetic storage devices. In either case, IBM would not be what it is today if it had stubbornly refused to give up the older technology.

Even though expert systems represent an augmentation rather than a replacement technology, many companies will not acknowledge it. Attempting to compete with expert systems, conventional programming techniques are being stretched beyond the point of diminishing returns. New, but conventional, products and applications are being introduced as AI applications when in reality they are only conventional applications in disguise.

Summary

The three trends discussed – technology evolution, technology diffusion, and technological discontinuity – dovetail to explain the current situation with expert systems. Enthusiasm has imparted a great deal of marketing top spin. Some companies heavily invested in conventional technology have resisted change and have responded by stretching, repackaging, and relabeling their older systems. These forgeries, as well as some of the true early applications, have produced disappointing results. Disenchantment has set in and the technology has been undervalued and underdeveloped.

In such a market, with many forgeries, caveat emptor applies. Both the forgeries and early imitative applications understandably appear comfortable, safe, and familiar.

Today's applications of expert systems are indicative of the imitation phase. Although the technology is innovative, the office process of analysis and decision making remains unchanged; the professional is just provided more support. Experimental uses to replace or change the process are just now beginning to enter our consciousness. As experience with expert systems increases, expectations will become both more realistic and innovative. Where this will lead is anyone's guess. Expert systems are coming out of their down cycle and expectations are rising to meet realistic capabilities. After years of publicity and development, few success stories are available. Lack of success stories has led to devaluation. The devaluation and the imitative approach has obscured the significance of the expert systems. Thus obscured, the nature of the technological discontinuity has not yet been realized.

The technological discontinuity created by expert systems can lower the cost of software development as well as increase the business benefits we realize from computerization. Expert systems have been sold as a replacement technology that displaces conventional approaches and can stand alone in a business environment. This is rarely the case. Expert systems are an augmentation technology that can be used to enhance and extend the capability of existing software. In many commercial applications conventional software is required to support and enable the effective use of expert systems.

The technology cycles that affect the user community also affect the vendors, except vendor cycles lead those of the user community. The vendors are responding and are quickly solving the main impediment to success: integration with conventional data processing. Success stories will multiply and stock in expert systems will rise. Positive experiences will lead to experimentation and the nature of the technological discontinuity will become apparent.

From the standpoint of conventional programming, expert systems have had an impact. Much of the work done at Xerox PARC has led to windows, graphics, and better user interfaces. The impact has gone farther than just personal computer applications. It has had a subtle affect on the thinking of almost every computer analyst responsible for developing user screens, regardless of the environment.

This is a learning process. Standards and norms become accepted because there is no other way; however, once a better way is found, the old standards are replaced. This process, in relation to expert systems, has also affected the way companies look at conventional applications. Some of the design, analysis, and development techniques used in expert systems are beginning to find their way into conventional environments. Knowledge mapping techniques can be used to improve data and control structures. Highly interactive development environments can lower system cost, improve quality, and speed development. Knowledge engineering interview techniques can be used to improve requirements definition and the user/analyst interface.

On the other hand, expert system technology has much to gain from conventional programming disciplines. Many application areas are not suited for expert systems and a great deal of time is spent in knowledge engineering to solve problems more appropriate for conventional programming techniques.

Section III

The Technology

7

Expert System Basics

Definitions

Precisely defining expert systems is a futile task because they are so fluid and amorphous. The Turing Test establishes a good definition for machine intelligence that could be adapted to expert systems. The test classifies a machine as intelligent if an observer cannot distinguish between the results produced by the machine and the results produced by a human. Similarly, this test would classify a system as an expert system if any observer could not distinguish between the results produced by the system and those produced by a human. This is a general test and trying to make it more specific only results in excluding desirable expert system examples. This is the case with the rule-inferencing definition introduced earlier that stated: "Expert systems are systems that employ rule-inferencing techniques."

As a derivative of the definition, one would correctly expect expert systems to contain both rules and inferencing capability. Consequently, the rebuttals to this definition would fill volumes. At a minimum, it excludes object-oriented systems, neural networks, and pure knowledge systems that don't use rules. But it's important to note that the rule-inferencing definition is not meant to define expert system technology. It only serves to define the subject of this book. Being congruent with common usage, it includes most commercial expert system applications.

Ideal applications for expert systems fall outside of the application areas for conventional computer systems. Expert systems are best applied to tasks where knowledge, experience, and judgment are key determinants of performance, though they can be applied to pure logic tasks. The primary requirement is that the task be analysis-like or decision-like. The term *task* is used to differentiate between process-oriented activities such as general management and task-oriented activities such as evaluating a credit risk once all of the required information has been collected. Process-oriented activities are far too broad and general to automate and require a level of reasoning ability beyond the capabilities of expert systems.

Tasks, on the other hand, are expert system candidates because they are specific and well bounded. Potential tasks could include:

Budgeting
Employee Evaluation
Applicant Screening
Underwriting
Credit Risk Analysis
Purchase Authorization
Claim Approval
Problem Diagnosis
Order Assembly
Fraud Detection
Risk Analysis
Complex Data Entry Editing

However, even the tasks listed above are too broad for expert system application, because the problem to be solved by the system must be highly specific. For instance, while budgeting and fraud detection are too broad, capital expense budgeting for computer equipment and fraud detection as part of a credit card purchase authorization system are specific enough to be implemented.

Usually expert systems are constructed using the knowledge of a single individual who is usually referred to as the domain expert. Knowledge acquisition is the process of identifying, defining, and organizing an individual's knowledge. Knowledge engineering includes the design and programming processes.

Since expert systems differ from procedural conventional systems that process transactions or records, some new terms are used to describe expert system concepts. Conventional system specifications are defined as algorithms that define the system's limits and capabilities. Such algorithmic specification is impossible with expert systems, so the system's limits and capabilities are defined by the knowledge contained in the system's *knowledge domain.* The knowledge domain in turn is defined as the knowledge required to provide the necessary analysis on *problems* or *cases* within the system's *problem domain.* These terms may seem a bit fuzzy and confusing but they do serve as a form of shorthand to communicate concepts. For example, the problem domain for a system used to provide approval for credit card purchases is defined as all of the different types of approval requests the system is to handle. The cases and problems the system handles are specific examples of requests within the problem domain. And finally, the knowledge domain describes all of the knowledge the system must have to successfully handle any case within its problem domain.

Expert systems can be used in a variety of modes, but most often they are designed to be a guide, assistant, counselor, or mentor to the system user. In addition to being able to handle knowledge and judgmental tasks, expert systems differ from conventional systems in that they can provide explanation capabilities. The explanation facility has many uses and can be a valuable training tool because it renders the system capable of explaining the reasoning behind its observations and recommendations. Since the explanation closely approximates the reasoning of the domain expert, it provides a user training capability that is consistent, patient, and ever-present.

System Basics

Throughout our lives we accumulate two types of knowledge: facts and heuristics. Facts are things we don't have to think about – they just are. Some facts about automobiles would be:

- Pintos are made by Ford
- My car's make is Pinto
- My car's color is brown

While simple facts are merely a matter of memory, heuristics require some logic and reasoning capability. Heuristics, sometimes referred to as *rules-of-thumb*, are the mental rules used to draw conclusions or make judgments about facts. In many cases, heuristics are so basic they are considered common sense and barely enter our consciousness. When used in everyday living they would generally be expressed in an unstructured form such as:

That's not my car – it's green – mine is brown.

This statement contains two facts – *The car is green* and *My car is brown* – and a declarative assertion – *That's not my car.* In expert systems, the above statement could be formalized into the following IF-THEN rule:

IF car color is not brown
THEN
car is not my car.

Since the car under discussion is green, the above rule would assert *the car is not my car*, and this new fact would be stored in memory. In this simplistic one-rule example, it takes little intelligence to pick the right rule and reach a conclusion. But since actual systems contain many rules and facts, some form of higher reasoning is necessary to control the process. This reasoning ability is referred to as the system's inferencing capability.

Expert systems must have the reasoning ability to select from the many facts and heuristics available those few that will produce the desired result. To demonstrate, the above rule is generalized and a few additional rules are added.

1. **IF car color is not my car color**
   THEN
   car is not my car.

2. **IF car make is not my car make**
   THEN
   car is not my car.

3. **IF car maker is not my car maker**
   THEN
   car is not my car.

Since the only thing we know about *car* is that it is green, the last two rules and their associated facts would be ignored. However, the first rule and its associated facts would combine to effectively produce the syllogism:

The car color is green and my car color is brown
Therefore
the car is not my car.

The knowledge and the reasoning components of expert systems are referred to as the knowledge base and inference engine respectively. The knowledge base contains programming statements that identify facts and rules. The inference engine, a computer program in its own right, controls the system's reasoning process by selecting and organizing the available knowledge in a way that produces a solution.

Figure 7.1 – Basic Expert System Model

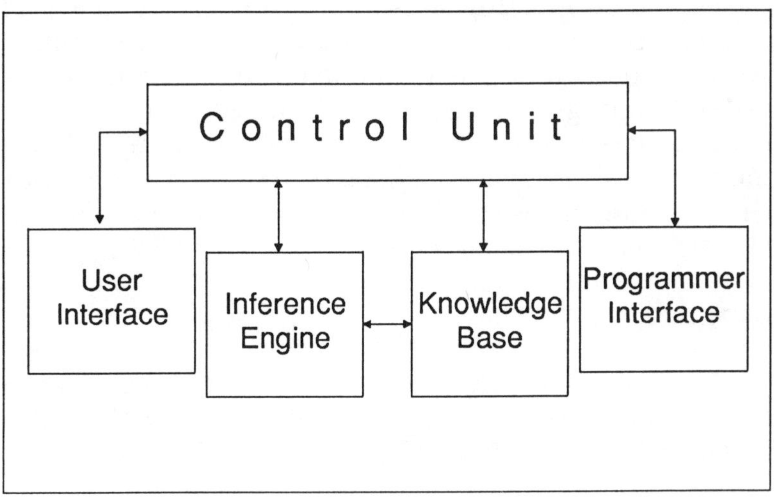

Although different applications require different knowledge bases, inference engines are generic so the same one can be used in many different applications. For a system to be useful, a user interface, a programmer interface, and a control unit are needed as shown in Figure 7.1. The interfaces allow users and programmers to communicate with the system, while the control unit governs all intercomponent interaction.

Development Tools

Expert system technology provides us with a cornucopia of techniques that allow us to cost effectively computerize human knowledge and expertise. Expert systems could have been built in earlier years using conventional programming techniques, but in most cases the cost would have been prohibitive, or the systems unmaintainable due to their complexity.

The computerization of knowledge and expertise is accomplished through the development of knowledge bases and supporting software to control interface and inferencing functions. Fortunately, vendor-supplied software packages are available that contain the computer languages, modeling techniques, and program control structures required for expert system development. These software tools come in a wide variety but can be categorized as languages, shells, hybrids, environments, and design tools.

Languages

Computer languages are the basic software development tool and almost seem too trivial to discuss, but two particular languages, LISP and Prolog, are worth noting. Systems can be built from the ground up using LISP or Prolog. Writing systems in these languages improves software portability from one type of computer to another. Using these tools, the inference engine, knowledge representations, and control structures can be developed to precisely match the application. Done properly, systems built with these tools will run faster and be more closely tuned to the user environment. However, development costs will be substantially higher because the development team will have to do a great deal of basic development. Before an expert system can be built using these tools, inferencing, control, and support software will have to be developed. As a rule, these tools will, at a very minimum, double or triple development costs. Development of systems using only languages should not be attempted without experienced and knowledgeable development staffs.

While both are popular expert system development languages, they have different characteristics. LISP is a lower-level language that gives the programmer a high level of control and flexibility. LISP is best suited for developing programmer tools; Prolog is best suited for building user applications. Because of this, most of the high-level tools discussed below were initially developed in LISP.

Shells

Shells can be considered an expert system without a knowledge base since they include the required inferencing, interface, and control structures. These tools are similar in concept to personal computer database packages such as dBASE II, R:BASE, and Lotus 1-2-3. These tools provide basic interfaces to other files and programs and can be used to develop stand-alone or integrated applications. Personal computer-based shells require limited technical expertise, and some can be used by non-technical personnel to develop their own applications.

Shell software provides everything needed to build a system. Software routines needed for knowledge representation, inferencing, recommendation explanation, and control are provided. System development can proceed rapidly but there is a trade-off. There are many different types of knowledge representation, rule structures, and inferencing techniques. Shells generally implement only a few of these. If the application under development fits well within the techniques supplied by the shell, there is no problem. However, if the application and the shell-supplied capabilities are ill matched, one of three situations can develop.

- Development costs increase because additional time is spent working around shell limitations. This can result in systems with less than an optimum design. System performance and maintenance suffer.

- The application flexibility and usefulness will be compromised to fit within the constraints of the shell.

- Application flexibility and capability can be so severely limited the development effort will fail.

Considering the improvement shells provide in development productivity, they are relatively inexpensive. However, flexibility and power are reduced because they provide limited problem solving, screen design, and reporting capabilities.

Hybrids

As used here, the definition of hybrid tools differs from that normally found in the expert system literature. Tools such as KES, OPS-5, M.1, and OPS-83 are normally referred to as "large narrow tools," but hybrid is more descriptive because they are a cross between a language and a shell. These specialized tools incorporate many shell functions, but provide more control and flexibility. In addition to rule constructs, the hybrids incorporate a high-level programming language that allows programmatic control of system functions normally preset in shell packages.

Design Tools

Conventional software development aids include a wide variety of Computer Aided Software Engineering (CASE) and programmer productivity tools. For expert systems, most similar tools are supplied as a component integrated with an expert system development tool. The most common are rule generators and programmer development aids.

Rule generators assist the development process by automatically generating rules for the programmer: either through induction or deduction. The former generates rules based on a set of examples, while the latter generates rules based on an intelligent computer-controlled dialogue with an "expert." Rule generators are relatively new and have limited use, but they are more than adequate for many applications.

Programmer aids used during program development include many different types of utilities, editors, and debuggers that are often coupled with graphic display capability.

Environments

Environments, a combination of all of the previous tool types, are at the high end of the expert system tool range. Tools such as ART (from Inference Corporation) or KEE (from Intellicorp) form a complete development workbench and are unsurpassed in flexibility, power, and programmer productivity. In one integrated development environment, programmers have available: a full array of programmer aids; direct languages access to handle detailed low-level functions; special high-level language constructs similar to those available in hybrid tools; and prepackaged functions and capabilities similar to those provided by shells.

Environments are appropriately called expert craftsman tool kits because they are for programming experts, and they provide the tools necessary to develop virtually any expert system within technical reach.

Tools and Overhead

Tool prices vary with shells being the lowest, environments the highest, and languages and hybrids falling in between. This is a general application of the rule that "you get what you pay for." However, one can also expect to "pay for what he pays for" in terms of limitations, staffing costs, project overhead, or increased computer requirements. At the low end, personal computer packages are simple and easy to use but lack flexibility. At the high end, environments are extremely powerful, but require specialized technical skills and increased computer power. User-built personal computer solutions may be adequate for some applications, but they can't compete with the larger applications requiring the more sophisticated tools. As with conventional systems, the proper balance depends on the application.

Tool Portability

Many of the software tools available today are the progeny of the doctoral dissertations and masters' theses of the late seventies. As a rule, they started out as a computer-specific tool for use only within the stand-alone, ad hoc application niche. A few years ago, the tools could have been grouped according to interface characteristics and computer compatibility. This is no longer the case because the vendors have capitalized on increasing computer power and software portability. With the dissolution of hardware and software boundaries, high-end LISP-based tools have moved to personal, mini, and mainframe computers, while the low-end PC-based tools have completed a corresponding upward migration.

8

Rule-Inferencing

Introduction

Some contend expert systems just represent a new way to program computers. This statement is true since in the final analysis, expert systems represent a subdiscipline of software engineering. However, the statement is overly simplistic because expert systems represent a conceptual change in approach. Saying expert systems are just another way to program computers is like saying calculus is another way to do math.

Each different type of computer application such as accounting, actuarial, or engineering utilizes different programming techniques. Even though different techniques are used, the fundamental numeric, procedural, and data-driven constructs are the same. One application, modeling the human decision process, has frustrated users of this conventional approach for years. The conventional approach has failed because it was designed to crunch numbers, move data, and make precise, clear-cut logic decisions. The conventional approach was not designed to handle the mechanics of human-like decisions where the fundamental constructs include judgment, knowledge, concepts, and fuzzy decision criteria.

To create expert system technology as we know it today, scientists not only had to confront the enigma of the human mind, but had to cut the software equivalent of the Gordian Knot. The human decision process is far too complex to program in conventional languages, and modeling the human thought process requires symbolic, nonprocedural programming techniques that further increase program complexity. So in cutting the Knot, scientists had to develop new approaches that employed software engineering to reduce complexity, while at the same time developing new nonprocedural, symbolic techniques. The two aspects of the solution, engineering and technique, are so interrelated they cannot be separated. However, software engineering will be discussed first because it is more fundamental.

Software Engineering

Program Complexity

The complexity of a computer program determines the upper limit of our ability to solve problems with computers. Complexity has two components: the complexity of application, and the complexity of the programming effort it takes to write the program. Application complexity is normally easy to recognize. For example, a program that reconciles a bank statement is less complex than a program that calculates the stress on an airplane wing. Or, a data entry/inquiry program is less complex than a program that makes judgments about credit risks. The complexity of the programming task is not as easy to measure and depends on the computer language used, the quality of the program design, and the nature of the available support tools. From the programmer's standpoint, the right language, support tools, and design can substantially reduce the complexity of the programming task.

In the previous sentence, *from the programmer's standpoint* is the operative phrase. Since programming is a human process, the human mind, not the computer, is the limiting factor. Computers are error free and can perform any task, regardless of complexity, once given the proper instructions. However, a program will certainly fail once it becomes so large and complex that programmers can no longer comprehend it.

System Modularity

There are two ways to manage program complexity. The first is to select the computer language and programming environment best suited to the type of application. The second is to employ sound software engineering principles.

Software engineering principles provide design guides to reduce program complexity. Intuition confirms that the simpler (i.e., less complex) the program, the easier it is to build, change, enhance, and maintain. The technique of dividing large programs into smaller programs, called modules, is one of the more important design techniques and is the foundation of structured programming techniques.

Normally large programs are divided into numerous smaller programs called modules each of which is designed to perform a specific function. If a program has only one module, then the definition of *module* and *program* are synonymous, and the size of the module is equal to the size of the program.

Figure 8.1 shows the relationship between complexity and the number of modules in a hypothetical 100,000-line program. As the number of modules increases, the average module size decreases, and the program becomes less complex. The two end points on the curve are both theoretical and intuitive. Intuitively, writing a 100,000-line program would be a very complex task, but writing 100,000 one-line programs would be comparatively simple although time consuming. Empirical testing can prove the curve's validity by asking any programmer two questions and plotting the answers.

Figure 8.1 – Program Complexity versus Number of Modules

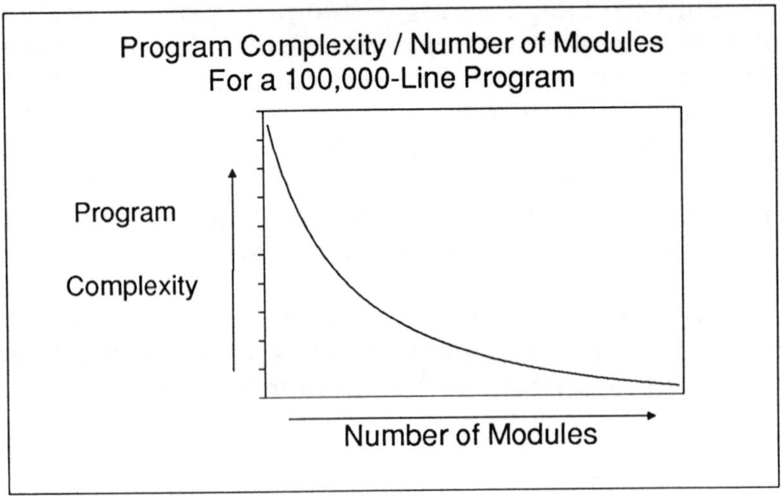

"If you wrote a program ten lines long, what is the probability it would operate error free without testing?"

"If you wrote a program ten thousand lines long, what is the probability it would operate error free without testing?"

Fortunately, the relationship between average module size and complexity is not linear. When the average module size is decreased 10%, overall program complexity is reduced by more than 10%. For example, if our hypothetical 100,000-line program is divided into ten 1,000-line modules, the total complexity of the ten modules would be less than the original program. However, the very act of dividing a large program into modules increases complexity because the modules are not totally independent because they must work together.

Since the modules cannot be totally independent, they require organization, and they must communicate and interface with each other. At a minimum, each module requires at least one interface and, as shown in Figure 8.2, each additional interface increases program complexity. Again, the curve is intuitive: if there are no interfaces, there can be no interface complexity; however, if there are a great number of interfaces, the system will be highly complex.

Figure 8.3 shows the two previous curves superimposed. The intersection of the two curves is the optimum design point that produces the lowest program complexity. Finding this design point is only the first

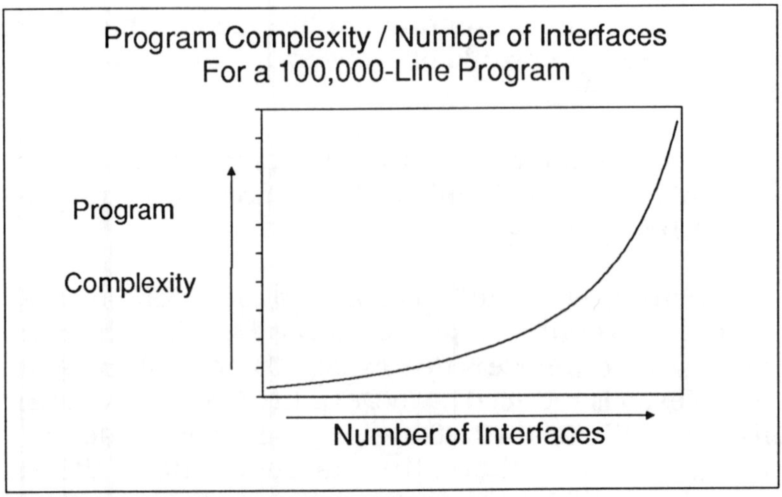

Figure 8.2 – Program Complexity and the Number of Interfaces

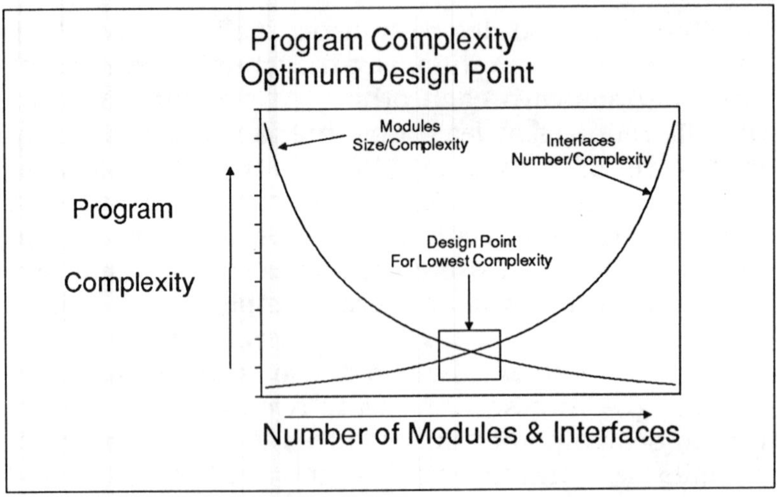

Figure 8.3 – Optimum Design Point For Lowest Complexity

step: three other interface related factors – knowledge, communication, and organization – must be considered.

For modules to work together there must be some formal organization, and each module must have some knowledge of the function, expected results, and information requirements of the other modules. Organization implies communication, which in conventional programming involves rigid data structures with known inputs, outputs, and data types. As a program grows in size it begins to behave like a large, complex bureaucracy that is inflexible and difficult to change.

Theoretically, we could develop a computer application of enormous complexity at a relatively low cost, if the application was written in very small modules that required no interfaces, organization, or communication paths. Unfortunately this is impossible, since modules must communicate and have some organization if any useful processing is to be done. However, computer languages can be developed to handle the interface, organization, and communication problems. If the languages handled these problems automatically for the programmer, something very close to the theoretical optimum would be achieved. Because a great deal of complexity would be hidden from the programmer, the programming task would be simpler, and more complex applications could be written. This is the approach taken by most expert system development tools.

Expert System Techniques

LISP

LISP is the most popular expert system development language because it is well suited to the type of programming tasks encountered. It eases the complexity management task in two ways. The structure of the language enforces good design techniques and the language handles many of the interface, organization, and communication problems for the programmer. However, the most important aspect of LISP is the way it handles data structures.

Conventional programming languages have dozens of different data types and structures. These languages require the programmer to precisely define and keep track of each data element and structure used. Even though we all know what a table of data is, and can conceptually adapt to any specific example (i.e., a parts list, price list, financial spreadsheet, sales report etc.), conventional programming languages do not allow this. Instead, they require the programmer to define the exact number of rows and columns as well as the type of data contained in each row and column. If the table changes slightly through the addition of a new row, column, or data type, the entire table has to be redefined. This type of programming characteristic is due to the explicit, numeric, and data-driven nature of conventional languages.

LISP allows programmers to deal with data structures symbolically at a conceptual level. Using LISP, a programmer could define a symbol *TABLE* and work with it at the conceptual level. Rows, columns, and data types could be moved, changed, added, and deleted at will without any programming intervention so long as the concept of *TABLE* is not altered.

LISP delivers this capability through a simple way of structuring data into lists. Lists are the only structure permitted, and a list can consist of a list of lists. The list data structure allows programmers to deal with large complex structures easily without having to be concerned about detail. For example, a program may have a list titled *DICTIONARY*. The programmer does not have to be concerned with the internal list details: he does not have to know how many entries it contains, the nature of the entries, or their organization. He can, for example, add another list *VERBS* to *DICTIONARY* with one simple command. Likewise, the program might contain a symbol referred to as *MILL*, which could contain a single definition or a list of definitions. To the programmer, *DICTIONARY*, *VERBS*, and *MILL* are symbols so a new verb definition for “mill” could be added without being concerned about data structures because the concepts involved are not affected.

The same result could be obtained using conventional languages but would require hundreds of lines of program code and probably several program changes to accomplish. In actuality, all of these changes are made in a LISP program, but LISP does it automatically for the programmer. LISP has this capability because of one other characteristic – it is an interpreted rather than a compiled language.

In a compiled language, all of the programming statements are deciphered and translated into computer binary code before the program is run, and can't be changed during program execution. Program statements written in an interpreted language are deciphered and executed (interpreted) while the program is running. This allows interpreted languages to dynamically modify data structures and even instructions while the program is running. This is a valuable capability. It reduces development time, especially in a prototyping environment, and as will be explained shortly, makes nonprocedural programming easier. The cost of this capability is longer execution times, and it places memory management beyond the reach of programmer control.

Rule-Based Programming

Rule-based programming is a technique that both models human thought and reduces complexity. In rule-based programming, the concept of *module* is replaced by *rule*. Each rule is a single programming statement with a unitary function. From a software engineering standpoint a rule is the smallest module possible. Rules look very much like the IF-THEN constructs used in conventional programming. Within an expert system, the rules are contained in a special part of the system called the knowledge base. A rule lies dormant until the conditions specified in the "IF" part of the rule exist. When the conditions are met, the rule becomes active (fires) and performs its function. Usually a rule's function is to make an assertion about some condition or value. In the act of assertion, a rule is adding information to a combined pool of other facts and assertions. If any combination of these conditions satisfies another rule, that rule fires, contributing to the problem solution.

The sequence in which the rules are written or stored in the knowledge base generally has no effect on the operation of the system. The use of rules does not require the programmer to set organization, structure, or procedure. In rule-oriented programming, the inference engine constructs a structure and procedure during execution.

The inference engine is the governing program and it also handles the organization, communication, message handling, and data management functions for the programmer. Because LISP treats everything as a list, including programs, a rule can be handled as either a small program or a small chunk of data. A rule can be inspected as data to ascertain its function, and then be executed as a program procedure. Being able to treat program procedures this way gives LISP a measure of introspective capability. LISP can not only execute a procedure, it can understand what it is executing. This allows the main LISP program to load a file containing many rules, determine which rules are eligible to fire, select those needed to solve the problem, and execute them in any order desired. Therefore, the sequence in which the programmer writes the rules does not establish the sequence of events nor problem-solving procedure. From the programmer's standpoint, programming is totally nonprocedural.

Rule-based programming represents a substantial step towards achieving the theoretically optimum programming language alluded to earlier. A rule is the smallest possible module and the inference engine automatically handles many of the factors that increase the complexity of the programming task.

- A rule knows nothing about any other rule in the system. A rule does not have to know which rule to access for information or what information other rules require.
- There is no organization, hierarchy, or set procedure. As the inference engine permits each rule to fire, the rule contributes some new information that may be required by other rules. The growing body of information creates a controlled chain reaction that produces the organization and procedure required to solve the problem. Programming is nonprocedural: the sequencing of events may be different every time. Since there is no structure, the rules are capable of multiple organizations to solve different problems.
- Rule-based programming reduces data structure and communication complexity. Within a rule, there is no data structure. External to the rule, no formal communication paths or structures exist.

The rule-inferencing approach not only reduces programming complexity, it also closely resembles the human decision process. One characteristic of the human mind is that it can adapt to different situations. The mind can adapt because it is nonprocedural and operates at an elementary level of facts and heuristics.

Given a particular problem, the mind seldom leaps to a preset procedure or formula. Instead, it combines known facts and heuristics to build a logic tree that leads to the ultimate conclusion. In effect, the mind creates (discovers) the procedure to follow that best fits the circumstances during the decision process.

In expert systems, the knowledge base represents the elemental knowledge – facts and heuristics. The inference engine emulates the human decision process by assembling the elemental building blocks of knowledge into a procedure tailored to the circumstances of the specific case under analysis.

Other Programming Assists

The human thought process presents other programming challenges. Typically human decision makers do not deal with a complete set of organized facts. Instead, they deal with fragmented evidence, indications, and clues. Expert system development tools provide built-in functions to handle missing information, uncertainty, and thresholding to help programmers develop systems that emulate human cognitive behaviors.

Missing Information

The conventional programming approach requires extensive data editing for the presence of data as well as data type and validity. At an extreme, a program may have to check each data item each time it is used. This would be a formidable task, especially in large systems with hundreds or thousands of data items.

Rule-based programming eliminates the missing data problem in a manner that emulates the way the mind deals with missing information. Rules do not fire unless certain conditions are true, and until data is present a condition is neither true nor false. So, if data is missing, it has no value and the rules dependent on it do not fire. In effect, the inference engine ignores what isn't there, and nothing happens relative to the missing data. If the missing information is vital, or a conclusion can be drawn based on the absence of information (i.e., "The applicant didn't want to answer that question because . . . ."), rules can be constructed to fire in these situations. The rule-inferencing construct operates much like a human would with incomplete information. If nonessential information is missing, it is ignored or conclusions are reached based on the fact that the information is missing.

Uncertainty

Often the human decision process is a matter of selecting the best solution from several alternatives. To reach a decision, the mind may have to explore several contradictory hypotheses by collecting and weighing evidence, some of which may be suspect. To model this process, expert systems need the capability to handle uncertainty and thresholding.

The way the mind deals with uncertain or suspect information can be modeled through mathematical probability. This facilitates the evaluation of multiple hypotheses based on the probability that the given information is true.

Uncertainty can be handled at the fact or the rule level. A suspect fact can be assigned a probability of being true or false. For example, a loan officer may conclude that a loan applicant's income of $30,000 is overstated. The loan officer is not concluding the number is wrong – he is only doubting its validity. In other words, the loan officer feels that the stated income has a low probability (i.e., 10%) of being true.

Probability can also be applied to measure the reliability of rules. Continuing the loan officer example, the loan officer may know that applicants with a particular demographic profile make good credit risks. Again, the conclusion is not that the applicant is a good credit risk, but that the conclusion is valid a high percentage (i.e., 90%) of the time. In this example, the facts about the applicant's demographics are the premises to the knowledge base rules. When these rules fire, the final conclusion is asserted as a fact with 90% certainty.

The two levels of handling uncertainty can be combined. The loan officer's final recommendation may depend on the result of two rules each indicating a different probability that the applicant is a good credit risk. If these two rules respectively yield a 75% and a 90% probability the applicant is a good credit risk, the final conclusion can be asserted with 96% certainty. (For an explanation, see the insert at the top of the following page.)

Thresholding becomes valuable in situations where the mind may avoid drawing any conclusions until almost certain about a particular situation. Thresholding occurs when the preponderance of the evidence leads to a conclusion. For example, if no conclusion is

> There are several methods used to combine confidence levels. This example explains one of the simplest.
>
> When combining confidence levels, the two probabilities that the statements are true cannot be simply multiplied to produce a 67.5% (0.9 X 0.75 = 0.675) confidence level. If we multiplied the probabilities that the statements are false (i.e. 10% and 25%), the result is 2.5%. Since the two probabilities must sum to 100% they are normalized. So,
>
> 67.5% / (67.5% + 2.5%) = 96.4% Probability of being True
>
> 2.5% / (67.5% + 2.5%) = 3.6% Probability of being False

possible until a certain fact is 90% certain, a thresholding situation exists. Before the threshold, the conclusion is neither true nor false, but once the 90% threshold is reached, a rule would fire asserting the desired conclusion.

Pattern-Matching Rules

Pattern-matching rules can be used for either heuristic or fact-based reasoning. Pattern-matching rules are a form of high-level reasoning about classes of problems. Usually, the IF portion of the rule references knowledge structures and the THEN portion of the rule produces a result based on the knowledge structure. For example, if a system was trying to determine the make and model of an automobile, only one simple rule would be required. The rule would in essence state, "Take all of the information available on the automobile, match it against all known knowledge about automobiles, and return the make and model."

In writing the pattern-matching rule, the programmer does not have to be concerned with any of the particulars of the problem. He does not have to know what information is missing or suspect, nor does he have to worry about how the search will be done. Again, the programmer is working at a conceptual level with the problem and is stating only the result desired. The power and flexibility of pattern-matching rules should not be underestimated from either a development or maintenance standpoint. In a large knowledge base, there may be dozens of different strategies that could be employed and dozens of facts that could be known or unknown about the problem. As a result, there could be thousands of different ways to solve the problem depending on the situation.

As a tool, a pattern-matching rule allows a programmer to accomplish in a few lines of code the same task that would require hundreds, if not thousands, of lines of code in conventional languages.

Meta-Rules

Meta-rules are rules that govern other rules. Using meta-rules, knowledge engineers can control certain aspects of the rule-inferencing mechanism. For example, in a knowledge base there may be different sets of rules, each designed to implement a particular problem solving strategy. If certain conditions are met, the knowledge engineer may, through the use of meta-rules, prioritize the sequence in which the rule sets are examined. In this way the knowledge engineer can control problem solving strategy and focus the inference engine on those rules that are most likely to produce the best solution in the shortest time.

Definitions

It is not uncommon for a computer system to be labeled as "not a *true* expert system" just because it does not handle missing information, uncertainty, thresholding or pattern-matching. This unfortunate practice is akin to throwing the baby out with the bath water and does not give the technology the credit it is due. More specifically, this is an all-or-nothing test that defines the technology in terms of its application. What if the application under development does not require uncertainty? Does this mean the technology should not be used at all?

9

Programming Impact

System Differences

Rules are expressed as IF – THEN clauses. All traditional languages have IF – THEN clauses and constructs, so what's the difference? There are several. First, traditional languages deal with the information given them at the transaction or record specific data level. Expert systems rules deal with information at the conceptual level. One rule in an expert system language might replace dozens or hundreds of IF – THEN statements in a traditional language.

Building an expert system in a traditional language using IF – THEN constructs would represent an intolerable control structure problem. Traditional languages are inherently procedural. The programmer must tell the system to "do this then do that," etc. If the sequence is wrong or slightly out of sync the program will not operate correctly. The logic tree in such a system could get quite complex, and would be almost impossible to test and maintain. If the analyst misunderstood the expert, or the expert forgot to tell the analyst something, the validity of the inflexible and precisely defined logic structure would collapse. To build systems this way would require a perfect understanding of the experts' knowledge. Experts rarely have a perfect understanding of their knowledge. Even if they did, it would be highly unlikely they could perfectly convey that knowledge to a knowledge engineer.

The rigid and inflexible logic structures of traditional systems also affect system performance. Because traditional systems are procedural, logic paths have to be followed step by step to their inevitable end. To this extent conventional programs are like automatons that mindlessly follow exactly the same procedure regardless of the circumstances. This approach precludes opportunistic reasoning that can find the simple solution if one exists.

In an expert system, a given unit of knowledge has several characteristics.

- It does not apply in all situations.
- Its use may be modified by other knowledge.
- It can have multiple relationships with multiple pieces of higher- and lower-level knowledge.
- Not all of the relationships can be discovered by analysis or knowledge engineering techniques.
- Each rule represents a separate independent unit of knowledge and does not depend on other rules to work properly.

None of the statements above would be true of an IF statement written in conventional languages.

The Pen Advisor

For example, consider a trivial expert system. In this example, pattern-matching rules will be ignored to prevent it from getting over-trivial. The purpose of the system is to advise a user what to do if a pen is not working properly. To do this, the system must first diagnose the problem to determine if the pen is broken or if the ink cartridge is dry. Once the problem is diagnosed, the type of pen, or whether the pen is guaranteed or refillable has to be determined. From this information, the system can provide correct advice. The first part of the system would be a problem Diagnosis Knowledge Base. This part of the system could be written as rules as follows:

```
If pen body is broken
    then
    diagnosis is broken

If (pen body is not broken
    or body status is unknown)
    and pen does not write
    then
    diagnosis is dry cartridge

If pen body is not broken
    and pen does write
    then
    diagnosis is nothing wrong

If (pen body status is unknown
    and pen writes is unknown)
    or (Pen body is ok
    and pen writes is unknown)
    or(Pen body status is unknown
    and pen does write)
    Then
    diagnosis is uncertain
```

The second part of the expert system, a Pen Knowledge Base would determine the type of pen or at least one of its characteristics (guaranteed or refillable). In this example, assume that all of the relevant facts about three different pens have been loaded in memory using a knowledge representation technique as follows:

	Pen 1	Pen 2	Pen 3
Brand Name	Brand A	Brand B	Brand C
Price	$20	$2	$0.25
Pen Guaranteed?	Yes	No	No
Pen Refillable?	Yes	Yes	No

This table is very easy for the mind to understand. Given specific information, we could quickly infer which type of pen was being used. Depending on the situation, a human could determine the writing instrument under discussion was Pen 1 from knowing any one of three facts – brand name, price, or guarantee – even if all other facts were unknown. However, the pen could not be identified just by knowing it was refillable. In real problems, information can be known or unknown. If we assume that any of the four facts about any of the pens can be known or unknown, there are 144 possible combinations of facts. (If the reader is so inclined, and has time to burn, he is invited to confirm the author's math. For those not so inclined, the derivation of the former number and others that follow are mercifully omitted because their derivation is not material to the current discussion. The numbers are important to the extent that they help describe a problem that will be solved shortly.) The human mind will not deal with all 144 possible combinations of facts but will apply logic to determine what is important. The table below shows the total number of possible logic paths that can be used to determine a fact about the pens.

	Pen 1	Pen 2	Pen 3
Brand Name	3	3	3
Pen Guaranteed?	3	3	4
Pen Refillable?	4	3	3

The third part of the system would combine information from the previous two sections to come up with the appropriate advice. For purposes of the example, assume that the following rules-of-thumb apply.

- Guaranteed pens can be returned to the manufacturer for replacement if the pen is broken.
- Pens like pen 3 are totally disposable and when broken or dried up are meant to be thrown away.

This final part of the system, an Advice Knowledge Base, would be written as a series of rules.

1. If pen is disposable
or (diagnosis is broken
and pen is not guaranteed)
then
Throw pen away

2. If Pen is guaranteed
and the diagnosis is broken
then
Return to manufacturer for replacement

3. If Pen is refillable
and the diagnosis is dry
then
Refill pen with new cartridge

4. If diagnosis is unknown
or (diagnosis is broken and guarantee is unknown)
or (diagnosis is dry and refillable is unknown)
then
No advice can be given

5. If diagnosis is nothing wrong
then
No advice is necessary

Taken at face value this expert system example would not demonstrate the difference between conventional and expert system programming techniques. The same facts and rules could be put into either a conventional or expert system and satisfactory performance achieved. However, lets take a look at what really happened.

In this example, there are 1,296 possible combinations of input data for three pens. Despite the 1,296 possibilities, a human expert, through logic, could find 67 different ways to solve the problem as summarized by the possible outcomes below:

- Throw Pen Away - 6 possible logic paths
  2 possible solutions each achievable 3 different ways.

- Return to Manufacturer - 3 possible logic paths
  1 possible solution achievable 3 different ways.

- Refill Pen - 12 possible logic paths
  2 possible solutions each achievable 6 different ways.

- Unknown Problem - 45 possible logic paths
  4 possible solutions achievable through 2, 3, 16 and 24 different ways.

- No Problem - 1 possible logic path
  1 solution achievable only one way.

In conventional programming, the logic path (algorithm) must be explicitly specified by the programmer as a sequence of instructions. In the above case, a brute force program could be written that solves the problem by virtue of its sheer weight or by placing heavy-handed restrictions on the data, the user, or both. A more elegant approach might be to write a program containing each of the 67 different logic paths – but how would the program determine which logic path to use? In either case, any piece of knowledge represented by an IF statement might have to be imbedded in several places in the program. This would make adding or modifying knowledge problematic due to its precise placement in multiple logic paths.

If a brute force approach was taken, its speed and computer utilization would be extremely sensitive to the number of pens in the pen knowledge base. If the number of pens were increased modestly to 6 or 12 the total number of possible combinations would increase from 1,296 to 3,696 and 13,689 respectively. If 67 different logic paths were written, the programmer would have to specify which one to use. To specify the best one to use the program would have to be opportunistic and look at the input data. That would result in a solution no better than the brute force approach. Either way, a conventional program would have to be sensitive to the data. As the total number of possibilities increase the program gets bigger, slower, and more complex.

The Diagnosis Knowledge Base consists of four rules. Each rule represents an independent piece of knowledge. That knowledge is not tied by structure or logic to either the Pen or Advice Knowledge Base.

The Pen Knowledge Base is the repository of information on pens. The information on the pens is presented in a straightforward manner. The pen knowledge base has one of three goals: determine if the pen is guaranteed, refillable or disposable. Once the pen knowledge base has information in it, the more sophisticated expert system tools will automatically take the information available and derive the desired information with little or no additional programming. For the programmer it takes no more programming to handle 1,000 pens than one pen. Again, no piece of knowledge about any pen is tied to the rules in the Advice or Diagnosis Knowledge Base.

The goal of the expert system is to provide advice. As such, the Advice Knowledge Base is the controlling knowledge. Through sophisticated programming techniques, the inference engine will examine the five Advice Knowledge Base Rules and the information available. It will pick the approach that looks most promising. One possible example might be as follows:

> If the pen is disposable this will result in the shortest, simplest solution, so a goal is established for the Pen Knowledge Base to determine if the pen is refillable or disposable. Under control of the inference engine, the Pen Knowledge Base will draw whatever inferences are required to determine the information. Assume that during this process it was discovered that the pen under consideration was not refillable and not guaranteed.
>
> Given this information, a human expert would immediately turn to diagnosing the problem because all other information needed was known. In a similar fashion, the inference engine would establish a goal for the Diagnosis Knowledge Base to determine if the pen was broken. Again under inference engine control, information would be accessed or requested and the appropriate rules fired. If the diagnosis returned was "broken," the inference engine would recognize that all conditions required to satisfy an Advice Knowledge base rule had been met. That rule would fire and provide the advice "Throw the pen away."

What has happened in this example is the inference engine dynamically constructed and executed one of the 67 possible solution paths without the programmer having to get involved. In effect, the inference engine took independent pieces of knowledge, and wrote and executed the algorithm that best solved the problem based on the information given.

The way the knowledge was accessed and used was governed by the inference engine and was dependent on the structure of the problem, not the structure of the program or the way the knowledge was stored. This approach is impossible with conventional languages since by the very fact that one IF statement follows another the program determines structure and establishes dependencies.

Another important aspect of the rule-inferencing technique is its adaptability to case-specific data. In conventional programming, the analyst would not even attempt to program each of the 67 different procedures. Instead the analyst would develop one general purpose algorithm. To make the algorithm work, the analyst would have to write the program to ask for all known information up-front regardless of its relevance. The opportunistic nature of expert systems allow programmers to write programs that are both more flexible and user-friendly.

The Five Generations

The preceding paragraphs covered the technical basics of expert systems from a software engineering standpoint. From this discussion three characteristics of expert system programming should be evident.

- From a programmer's standpoint the programming of rules is inherently nonprocedural. The inference engine, not the programmer, will determine the exact sequence of events.

- Programming is elevated to a higher level of abstraction with the programmer dealing with symbols and concepts rather than detail data items and procedures.

- The built-in functions provided by the tools and the programming constructs used hide a great deal of complexity from the programmer by transferring a large part of the programming burden from the programmer to the computer.

The first two represent a change in programming approach away from the numeric procedural methods; the third represents how the change in approach is accomplished. These changes can be summarized and placed into context by reviewing the five computer generations.

The five generations refer to the nature of the programming languages in use. The five generations are:

- Binary
- Assembler language
- High-level languages such as COBOL, Fortran, etc.
- Declarative languages such as report writers and query languages
- Artificial intelligence techniques

In the first generation, programmers were required to program computers in binary, one instruction at a time. Binary programming placed the entire burden of problem definition and translation on the programmer. The computer architecture, not the nature of the problem, determined the structure and syntax of the language. No programming automation existed; the programmer was responsible for programming even the most trivial detail. Besides being time consuming, binary programming was tedious, complex, and fraught with error. The complexity inherent in the language confined programming to small, simple problems.

The second generation, Assembler language, contributed two improvements. Easy to remember mnemonics replaced binary instructions. So rather than entering an instruction as a cryptic sequence of numbers such as –

0101,1011,0001,1010,0111,1111,0101,0011

it could be entered as –

ADD,1;TAX

The second generation also introduced macro language capability that allows programmers to write and catalog common routines for reuse in other programs. Both characteristics made the Assembler language programming less complex and easier to tailor to the nature of the application. The programmer had to do less work because the computer started to carry a portion of the programming burden.

In the third generation, higher-level languages shifted more of the translation burden to the computer. The computer languages moved closer to natural human thought in two ways: First, by taking on natural language characteristics such as subjects, verbs, objects, and rules of syntax, the languages moved to a higher level of abstraction further removed from binary computer code. Second, languages like Cobol, Fortran, and PL/1 were specifically designed to simplify program development for certain types of applications.

Declarative languages, sometimes called nonprocedural languages, make up the fourth generation. These languages represent another step forward in programming abstraction. Rather than having to tell the computer how to accomplish a task, the programmer need only specify the result desired. Many fourth generation languages contain some third generation components, but again at a higher level of abstraction. These components represent a high-level programming capability that allow programmers to perform complex but specialized tasks with simple programming statements.

In some ways, AI, the fifth generation, breaks from previous trends. The first four generations could be distinguished by the constructs and characteristics of the language, but the approach to programming remained basically the same. Program organization, procedure, and data structures required explicit definition and remained fundamentally unchanged. The fifth generation takes a different approach.

Because the fifth generation focuses on the approach to programming rather than the nature of the language, defining the fifth generation in terms of languages would be an serious error. Fifth generation applications can be developed using second, third, or fourth generation languages. The languages and tools commonly used to develop expert systems can be roughly grouped into the first four generations. LISP and Prolog resemble third generation languages. Expert system shells resemble Lotus 1-2-3 and PC database packages, examples of fourth generation languages. The expert system hybrid and environment tools provide an integrated environment of third and fourth generation languages. All of these represent the fifth generation. What is unique about them is not the nature of the language but the way they approach programming.

With these caveats, the fifth generation does continue the patterns established in the third and fourth generations. The languages and techniques were specifically designed to simplify development of a particular type of application – modeling the human thought process. Fifth generation approaches help manage the complexity problem by transferring an enormous part of the programming burden to the computer.

Figure 9.1 summarizes programming task responsibility, by generation, based on standard programming tasks. For purposes of summary, it is assumed that the fifth generation shown in the figure is synonymous with expert systems. In the figure, the design and detail specification are developed by the computer. This does not mean, as some believe, that expert systems do not have to be designed. The figure displays what happens at the micro level; macro-level design is still required to produce quality software.

Task	Computer Generation				
	First	Second	Third	Fourth	Fifth
Feasibility Study	Programmer	Programmer	Programmer	Programmer	Programmer
Requirements Definition	Programmer	Programmer	Programmer	Programmer	Both
Design	Programmer	Programmer	Programmer	Both	Both
Detail Specification	Programmer	Programmer	Programmer	Computer	Computer
Compile	Programmer	Programmer	Computer	Computer	Computer
Assembly	Programmer	Computer	Computer	Computer	Computer
Binary Execution	Computer	Computer	Computer	Computer	Computer

Figure 9.1 – Programming Task Responsibility by Generation

10
Knowledge Engineering

Expert systems are more than just software and programming tools. By far, the most important aspect of expert systems is the skills to use the tools of the technology properly. Collectively, the skills are referred to as *knowledge engineering*, and as the title implies, the skills revolve around knowledge.

Knowledge

The value of a database to an organization depends on the quality, quantity, and accessibility of the data it contains. The same is true for expert systems if we substitute *knowledge* for *data*. Knowledge, not software, is the most important aspect of expert systems because the finest software and most sophisticated development techniques are worthless if the knowledge base is inadequate.

Knowledge Organization

It is thought that the mind stores knowledge as clusters of information centered around a symbol or concept. The knowledge stored in a cluster can contain information or links that point to other related clusters. For example, the knowledge cluster for symbol *bird* may contain general information about birds such as they fly, and have two legs, two wings, and one beak; and pointers to specific types of birds such as wrens, robins, and penguins. The links point to clusters that contain more specific information such as the characteristics unique to wrens. As we learn, the network of clusters becomes more complex as new clusters, more information, and new links are added. The linking of clusters allows us to quickly sift through our knowledge and reach conclusions like: birds are not mammals, a cardinal is a warm-blooded bird, a cardinal can refer to a bird or a baseball player. As commonly used in AI research, an expert is an individual who has the eight to ten years of experience it takes to accumulate 50,000 to 100,000 knowledge clusters about a particular subject.

Compiled Knowledge

As the knowledge clusters grow in size and complexity, the mind begins to create high-level clusters so we can quickly retrieve information about entire cluster structures without conscious effort. The high-level clusters represent a concept and the low-level clusters represent all that is known about that concept. The knowledge contained in the high-level clusters is referred to as *compiled knowledge*. Compiled knowledge is evident when listening to the conversation of two experts; they speak in shorthand using single words to communicate complex concepts that both understand, but neither has to think about.

Compiled knowledge can also be observed in the many decisions we make without really understanding the rationale. Over years, the human mind compiles knowledge in the form of patterns. When the mind encounters a pattern, the pattern is seldom recognized as such, but the compiled knowledge enters the decision process as a hunch, gut feeling, intuition, instinct or some other subconscious assertion.

We have all experienced this type of compiled knowledge when we have met someone new and reached a first impression. We do not know why we liked or disliked the individual, but we just have a feeling about them. We have identified a pattern of dress, deportment, voice, eye contact, or method of speaking and reached a conclusion. The exact combination of factors we have learned from experience is hidden, only the conclusion reaches our consciousness.

Knowledge Acquisition Challenges

Knowledge acquisition is part of knowledge engineering and is analogous to developing the detailed specifications for a conventional system. The purpose of knowledge acquisition is to identify, document, and organize the needed knowledge either through reference research or by working with an expert to help him articulate his knowledge.

Knowledge acquisition is the single biggest problem in expert system development. Because knowledge is unorganized and often hidden by compiled knowledge, knowledge acquisition is a discovery process, and often the more that is discovered the more there is to learn. Whether a system contains 50 or 5,000 rules, the problems are the same, only their magnitudes differ.

Specifying and identifying the knowledge required for an expert system has two components: scope and depth. The scope of a knowledge base relates to the number of subjects, or knowledge topics, the knowledge base must contain to provide the analysis or decision-making capability desired. The depth of the knowledge relates to the amount of knowledge required within each subject area. Taken together, the depth and scope of the knowledge base define the knowledge domain for the application.

The knowledge engineer must deal with many interpersonal, psychological, and motivational factors to establish a good rapport with the expert. Besides being a highly interpersonal process, knowledge acquisition presents many knowledge-related problems to the knowledge engineer, especially when the application calls for judgment rather than clear-cut answers.

Identifying Knowledge

In conventional system development, one of the first steps is to define what the application will do and bound the scope of the application. Since conventional systems deal with precise problems, needs, and procedures, they can generally be defined with a high degree of completeness and precision.

However, expert systems are another matter because knowledge about a subject is generally a mystery, even to an expert. Knowledge is not stored in outline form in neat mental volumes easily retrieved and examined. Instead, knowledge is highly interrelated and is retrieved based on the situation or some other external trigger. Because of this, it is difficult for us to know what we know in a way that allows us to summon all of our knowledge about a subject on request.

It is because of this characteristic of knowledge that knowledge acquisition is a discovery process. Knowledge must be collected and tested against real situations. Often the testing will present an unanticipated problem that points to a new area of knowledge.

This process is analogous to the way we teach other people how to handle job-related tasks. We begin by explaining as much as we can remember about the task at hand, and the new employee uses that knowledge until a situation arises that doesn't seem to fit what he has been told. Confronted by a specific example, we respond with "I forgot to tell you about . . . " and we then explain how to handle the new situation. This process occurs quite naturally, and is repeated until the new employee has mastered all aspects of the new task.

Defining the Knowledge Domain

Another aspect of identifying knowledge is defining the limits of knowledge required. At first blush it may seem easy to define the scope of knowledge required to solve a problem. But knowledge is highly interconnected. Knowledge on one subject leads to knowledge on another subject, and so on.

For example, an initial assessment of the knowledge required to evaluate commercial loan applications may specify that the knowledge base has to have knowledge and/or the ability to reason about:

- Financial condition of the borrower,
- Knowledge about the borrower's industry,
- Lender's policy,
- Reputation and track record of the borrower,
- Purpose of the loan, and
- Revenue sources to be used to repay the loan.

Once knowledge acquisition begins it may be discovered that loan officers consider product competition in the borrower's industry including potential foreign competition. Does this mean new topics about products and international competition have to be added to the knowledge base? Further knowledge acquisition may reveal the evaluation of large long-term loans includes inflation and labor costs pointing to new portions of the knowledge base on expected future economic trends.

Left alone, the scope of the knowledge base can expand continuously until it is impossible to implement. Controlling the scope can be difficult and it often requires making trade-offs and judging when enough is enough.

Knowledge Correction

Knowledge acquisition is not merely an organization and documentation process. Often knowledge requires correction and refinement. In situations where there is a clear-cut answer this is not a major problem, but the farther knowledge acquisition delves into compiled knowledge and areas of judgment, the more important the correction process becomes. A few of the knowledge correction problems that can occur are discussed below.

Textbook Knowledge

Often the way we explain how to analyze a situation reflects the way we think we should make the decision; however, the way we deal with actual situations is quite different. The explanation represents textbook knowledge, whereas the way we deal with the actual analysis represents expertise. This is what separates the beginners from the experienced pros.

Factor Importance

Related to the problem of textbook knowledge is the matter of determining the importance of decision criteria. When a decision is dependent on several different criteria, the importance of each factor must be identified and then integrated into a unified decision. Often what we think is important turns out to be almost insignificant in actual practice. How many times have we approached a major decision such as the purchase of a home or automobile and had our prioritized list of criteria virtually ignored when the final decision was made? One experienced knowledge engineer stated that it seems that the stated importance of a particular item is almost the inverse of its actual importance.

Conflicting Knowledge

One common, tricky problem that requires diplomacy is resolving conflicting knowledge and evidence. Often an expert may state his knowledge one way, review it, and agree with it; and then be presented with an actual example in which he made a decision contrary to what he has said. Was he wrong then, or is he wrong now? Either way, the problem must be resolved.

Knowledge Acquisition Process

There are many different schools of thought on knowledge acquisition, and methods vary in the level of structure and formality.

Formal Approaches

The most formal, highly structured, and thorough approaches will produce the best results. The formal approaches place a great deal of emphasis on removing interpersonal and motivational barriers, as well as on documentation and verification of knowledge.

One formalized approach can be viewed as a four-phase process of planning, interviewing, reviewing, and testing. The four steps are not rigidly executed in sequence; instead the process interleaves the four steps and repeats them until the desired results are obtained.

The first step in knowledge acquisition is to identify the subject areas that require investigation. The identified subject areas form the beginning of a knowledge outline that is used as a guide for subsequent knowledge acquisition.

Based on the outline, the expert is interviewed on each subject area to flesh out the outline until the knowledge is complete. So the knowledge engineer can focus on leading the interview and pay close attention to what is being said, the interviews are normally tape recorded so notes do not have to be taken. The interview tape transcriptions are far superior to notes because they are more complete and reflect what the expert said, not what the knowledge engineer thought was said. These transcripts, which form the basis for knowledge engineering, are used by the knowledge engineers to identify and organize the expert's knowledge.

Once the information contained in the transcripts is sifted and organized, rules, facts, and heuristics are identified and converted to a form of pseudo-code easily understood by the expert. The pseudo-code is a very concise and exact statement of the knowledge which is reviewed and verified with the expert. If the expert disagrees, the verbatim transcript can be reviewed to determine:

if the knowledge engineer misunderstood,

if the expert misunderstood the interview question,

if the expert misstated the facts,

or if the expert answered the question within the context of the interview and now something else has occurred to him that points to additional knowledge.

After review and revision, the pseudo-code is translated into rules and entered into the knowledge base for actual testing.

Prototyping is a development method ideally suited for ill-defined or ill-understood problems such as knowledge and decision processes. In these situations, it is difficult for individuals to state what they want, but it is easy for them to recognize it once they see it, or state what is wrong when presented with an example. The prototyping process not only helps define the knowledge, but when used with test cases helps identify knowledge errors, gaps, and needed refinements. If potential knowledge errors are identified, the rule(s) in question can be traced back to the pseudo-code and then to the transcript to identify the exact nature of the problem. The tight linkage between what the expert said and the actual system rules forms a knowledge audit system that helps insure that the knowledge is correct and complete.

The formal approaches are very time consuming for development personnel, but utilize the expert's time very effectively and produce very comprehensive, verifiable, and well-designed knowledge bases.

Informal Approaches

The most informal of approaches skips the planning, interviewing, and reviewing steps and focuses solely on prototyping. In this approach, a few basic rules are entered into the knowledge base and testing begins. This approach requires that the expert and the knowledge engineer work side-by-side at a terminal, and each time a test case fails, the expert is questioned and new rules added. This process continues until the system can properly handle all test cases.

The informal approaches such as this do not use an expert's time effectively, ignore knowledge base design, and produce knowledge bases that are difficult to measure and quantify. Nevertheless, informal approaches can be used on small, simple, noncritical applications where ongoing maintenance is not an issue.

Knowledge Characteristics

Based on the formal definition of an expert – eight to ten years of experience – it is clear an expert's knowledge can only be represented by a complex network of facts, logic, and heuristics. Building an expert system to replicate such an individual's knowledge would require the most sophisticated development tools and the most formal knowledge acquisition techniques. However, such expertise is not a requirement for an expert system application and the term *expert* may only confuse the issue.

Rather than deal with the term *expert*, it is more convenient to discuss knowledge characteristics in terms of clerical, paraprofessional, and professional tasks. Although the boundaries are only approximate, an individual should be able to become competent in a clerical task within one to two years, a paraprofessional task in one to five years, and a professional task in a minimum of four years. The groupings are convenient because the length of time it takes to become competent is some indication of the quantity and complexity of the knowledge involved in completing the task. In turn, these approximate knowledge characteristics can be used as guides to determine the appropriate software tools and knowledge acquisition techniques.

Clerical

The knowledge used in completing clerical tasks will probably be dominated by simple fact structures and logical statements. Judgment which requires handling uncertainty, probability, and thresholding will be basic, if used at all.

These types of tasks are easily implemented using personal computer shells and require only rudimentary knowledge engineering skills. Applications in this area can be developed by personnel new to expert systems with basic knowledge engineering training.

Structured knowledge acquisition skills are advisable, but the most effective techniques resemble conventional system analysis.

Paraprofessional

Paraprofessional tasks are likely to require moderately complex knowledge structures of much greater depth and breadth that are a balance between facts, logic, and judgment. Such applications can be implemented using shells, hybrids, or environments. Hybrids and environments are more appropriate at the high end, and shells adequate at the low end.

Paraprofessional applications require a higher level of knowledge engineering skills and should be approached cautiously by individuals with less than a year of expert system development experience. Additional experience is required if hybrid or environment tools are used for development. Knowledge acquisition techniques are likely to be a blend of system analysis and formalized knowledge acquisition.

Professional

Professional tasks require highly complex knowledge structures and heavy use of judgment in the reasoning process. With a few exceptions, professional applications are beyond the technical reach of personal computer shells unless carefully limited and structured. These applications are more appropriate for the hybrid and environment tools. Professional level applications should only be attempted by highly skilled knowledge engineers. For these applications, highly formalized knowledge acquisition techniques are required to acquire, organize, and verify the extensive and complex professional knowledge.

Knowledge Engineering Skills

Most of the personal skills and traits necessary for a good knowledge engineer are the opposite of those required to be a good conventional programmer. While both require good interpersonal skills to work with users, the programming, design, and analysis skills are quite different.

Conventional programmers are taught to define an application completely before they begin design, analysis, and programming. Conventional software is extremely unforgiving – loose ends, less than air-tight procedures, inexact logic trees, imprecise programming statements, or loosely designed and specified data are all things guaranteed to lead to program problems. Through training and experience good programmers learn to instinctively make sure everything fits in a clearly defined box and force closure on all open issues.

Conversely, expert system development, principally knowledge acquisition and prototyping, is a discovery process. If programmers force closure on open issues, important knowledge may be missed that will induce system errors or limit capability. Inexact logic and imprecise statement are the vehicle of human judgment and expertise, so trying to quantify them can negate the entire purpose of the system. Trying to tightly define data and procedures is not only extra work, but defeats the prototyping process and the purpose of the technology. In effect, the objective of knowledge engineering is to develop the specifications that yield the final system in the form of the final prototype.

Programmer Cross-Training

For individuals just entering the computer profession, learning to become a knowledge engineer requires training and skill development. For conventional programmers it requires training, de-programming, and skill development. De-programming is usually necessary to break the analysis, proceduralization, and definition habits ingrained in every programmer from his first day on the job. Training is generally not enough because in some cases the differences in approach are subtle and are difficult to learn without practice and skilled guidance. Companies who have not fully understood this point have produced many disappointing "expert systems" that in the final analysis were nothing more than conventional systems written in an expert system language.

With proper training and guidance, a conventional programmer with relational database experience can acquire the prerequisite skills for rule-based programming in about six months. If more advanced techniques such as frames, schema, and objects (not covered in this text) are employed, the conceptual leap for the programmer is larger and another three to six months of training are required.

At least one individual attempted to define expert systems as systems written by knowledge engineers. Depending on how one views the definition, it is either childish or profound since a technology can't be defined by job titles. But making good use of expert systems depends more on the skill of the builders than on the tools they use.

11
Foundation Benefits

Expert systems are a composite of software and knowledge engineering techniques which were touched on in the previous chapters, but there is still one piece missing from the puzzle – the nature of the tools used to build expert systems and how the pieces come together at the programming level.

Prototyping Tools

Most expert system applications are developed using shells, hybrid, or environment tools. Many of the functional requirements for these tools were determined by the needs of the programmer, not the final system user. The model environment used to specify the tools was heavily influenced by the stand-alone, ad hoc application research and development of the seventies. To many vendors the term *user-friendly* refers to the programmer, not the end-user, because the programmer is seen as the user who needs a prototyping environment that is easy to use, flexible, and powerful.

Without a productive prototyping environment, the rule-inferencing techniques would be difficult to employ and knowledge acquisition, testing, and refinement would be almost impossible tasks. As such, the prototyping nature of the tools represents the third key ingredient in expert systems technology. Whereas software engineering lowers program complexity by hiding complexity and performing a great deal of work for the programmer, and knowledge engineering skills allow us to mine the expert's knowledge and properly apply the software engineering techniques, the prototyping tools bring the two together in a productive environment. If any of the three ingredients were missing, expert systems would probably not be commercially viable.

The prototyping nature of the tools explains, to some extent, the integration and production problems. In the stand-alone, ad hoc application development environment, integration, response time, and highly efficient production user interfaces are not an issue.

Technical Capability

Expert system technology is neither a product nor a commodity. One cannot go down to the local computer store and buy a box of expert system technology. However, the tools and the skills of the technology can be acquired. The tools and the skills do not directly provide business benefit; they must first be applied to a business problem or opportunity. At the programming level, the technology provides several new or improved technical capabilities. In the application of the technology, these capabilities are the foundation benefits on which business benefits can be built.

General Benefits

Expert systems are commonly advertised as being most appropriate for decision and analysis applications where judgment and expertise are important. However, in developing a technology of sufficient power to handle these applications, scientists have produced a set of tools that have a broader application than their original target. Just as expert systems can be applied to clerical tasks, expert system techniques can be applied to smaller programming problems.

Before discussing these, a word of caution. Expert system technology is not a replacement technology: It is not the universal solution to every programming problem. One consequence of the nonprocedural nature of expert systems is that it is extremely difficult to make them behave procedurally. Most of today's computer applications are highly procedural and should not be considered as expert system candidates. This does not mean that expert systems cannot be used as an augmentation technology to provide assistance at specific isolated points within the procedural framework of conventional applications.

Development of Specifications

Some expert system specialists view the prototyping process as the development of system specifications, with the final prototype being placed into production or rewritten into another language. This view points to a valuable, but often overlooked, use of expert system technology. The technology provides the tools to unravel complex decision and logic processes that may or may not be dependent on expertise or knowledge.

In some applications, the knowledge acquisition and prototyping process will yield a highly structured decision tree and an understanding of the decision process that would have been impossible to attain using other methods. If a highly structured decision tree is discovered, it can be tested, verified, and translated into conventional languages.

Lower Development Cost

Using expert system technology as a programming tool for complex logic systems is a minor variation on the previous use. Just as programmers enjoy the productivity increases of using expert system tools for developing decision systems, so can they be enjoyed when expert system tools are used as a fourth generation programming aid on complex logic applications. These applications are not normally considered good expert system applications because they do not require judgment, uncertainty, or heuristic capabilities. If the intent is to demonstrate the capability of the technology, picking applications that require these capabilities is important. However, if the intent is to reap a business benefit from the technology the needs of the application should drive the selection of the technical tools, not vice versa.

System Maintainability

Computer systems tend to grow in complexity over time, and as they age they can become so costly to maintain the only viable option is to rewrite the system. Because of the software engineering techniques employed, and the nature of the tools, using expert system technology can ease both the development and maintenance burden.

The importance of the maintainability of expert systems should not be underestimated. A major asset of expert systems is their ease of maintenance relative to conventional approaches. Maintenance is a constant process of change, correction, and enhancement. Prototyping, which is what most expert system development tools were designed for, is a maintenance process except it is more intense and compressed than normal maintenance. Even in cases where clean logic paths exist, it may not make sense to implement the system in a conventional language if future maintenance requirements are a concern. Despite these glowing words about the maintainability of expert systems, the technology has not come to grips with long-term maintainability. As will be discussed in Section IV, improved maintainability is not a de facto benefit of expert system techniques.

Improved User Interfaces

Conventional applications tend to be highly structured, unforgiving, and inflexible in approach. A user may know there are five ways to complete a task, but the computer system is programmed to handle only one because it does not have the intelligence to select the method most appropriate for the situation. Because expert systems can sometimes infer missing data and are opportunistic, they can be used to augment, streamline, and improve user interfaces.

Foundation Benefits

Alternative Approaches

All of the general benefits above represent an alternative approach to existing technical problems – specification, development, maintenance, and user interface design. However, these alternative approaches are peripheral to application development. Expert system technology can be used to provide an alternative approach to entire applications.

Conventional computer limitations have resulted in some applications where the solution to the problem was molded to fit the capability of conventional programming techniques. For example, some statistical applications may require a great deal of data and computer resources to provide the same information a professional could provide with much less data and effort. Wherever the solution was molded to the existing computer capability in lieu of logic and reasoning, expert systems are likely to help.

New Applications

The most important technical capability delivered by the technology is the realm of new applications it makes possible. These applications, which are characterized by judgment or complex logic, are possible because of the technology tools that allow us to capture, codify, and computerize knowledge. Expert system technology makes two types of new applications possible.

First, applications dependent on professional experience, knowledge, judgment, and decision making are now within both technical and economic reach. Second, simpler clerical and paraprofessional applications that were within technical reach are now within economic reach because of new tools and techniques.

Knowledge Capture

Knowledge capture is the keystone of the three foundation benefits. The rule-inferencing, knowledge engineering, and prototyping techniques combine to allow us to capture, correct, codify, and computerize knowledge. Without the ability to capture knowledge, the new applications and alternative approaches would not be possible.

Summary

If we summarize the technical capabilities of the technology, the three foundation benefits become evident. These capabilities, which allow us to use alternative approaches, develop new applications, and capture knowledge, are the technological discontinuities that alter both the cost and benefit equations.

First, in specific situations expert system technology creates a replacement technology discontinuity by providing improved alternative approaches to old problems such as program maintenance, specification, and user interfaces. Second, at a more general level expert systems represent a parallel technology discontinuity by enabling the development of a new class of applications that are beyond the point of diminishing returns for conventional technology. Since the technology is targeted at a different class of problems characterized by the human thought process, it parallels, but does not replace, conventional approaches. Finally, the two previous benefits depend on the last, and most important benefit – the ability to capture, codify, store, and distribute knowledge.

Section IV

Development

12

Theory & Practice

Introduction

The extant theory on expert system development was formulated in the seventies and refined during the early eighties. The theory, as proffered by many AI experts, centers on stand-alone ad hoc applications and is strongly influenced by the technology's research heritage. The theory is heavily dependent on prototyping; views expert systems as a replacement rather than an augmentation technology; and by implication defines expert systems as a total and complete solution. Because of the stand-alone ad hoc application bias, the theory concentrates solely on expert system technology; excludes integration with conventional software systems; and dismisses conventional software development techniques as unnecessary, inappropriate or useless. The theory, when applied to commercial applications, fails to anticipate several important points.

- Development theory follows the academic research process of propose, research, prove, and then apply research findings. This process separates the problems of development from the problems of delivering the technology to end users.

- The theory is still heavily influenced by the work done in the late seventies and early eighties. During this period the primary purpose of development was to prove capability, not to deliver it. When the AI industry discovered the delivery problem in 1986 and 1987, integration became the buzzword in the industry. However development methods have not been updated to reflect this new requirement.

- Just as the theory does not anticipate the development problems associated with delivery, it does not anticipate the problems associated with maintaining systems once delivered.

- The development theory concentrates on expert system tools and techniques excluding integration and conventional approaches. This dangerous, myopic view ignores practical experience indicating that the effort expended in conventional software development will equal, or exceed, the knowledge engineering effort for most integrated expert systems.

Each of the above points are symptomatic of an emerging technology that has not yet reached full commercialization. The basic problem is that the purpose of expert system development is changing. Building demonstration systems where delivery and maintainability are not important is not the same as building maintainable end user systems. As the purpose changes, so do the requirements, and so must the development methods and techniques.

The technologists are quick to point out they are just talking about the expert system component of the final application. They are correct, but seldom is this point made, nor is it indicated there are other concerns. Through repetition and wide dissemination, their view has been accepted as unquestionable fact, and dogmatically transferred from the research to the commercial arena. The technologist's view of development has become so pervasive, even those who should know better can be easily seduced.

System Theory

Figure 12.1 is the expert system model introduced in chapter seven. The model is accurate for any single user applications where the expert system has direct control over the user interface and interfaces to other computer applications are not necessary. The model represents a totally self-contained application and is indicative of a replacement rather than an augmentation technology model. The model in Figure 12.1 is significant because it is the basis for popular development theories, but it applies to only a small fraction of potential business applications.

Development Theory

Figure 12.2 is a composite of several popular expert system development models used by many authorities to explain system development. After the first two preliminary steps, the development process is roughly divided into three stages: propose (demonstration prototype); research/prove (prototype); and apply (delivery porting and release).

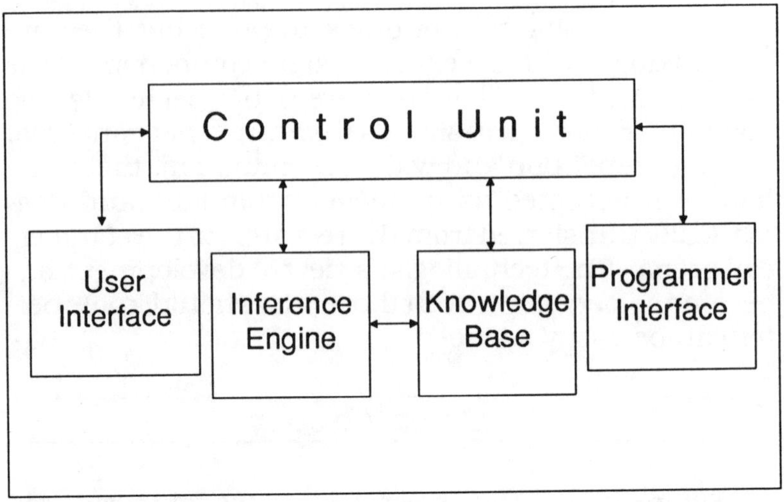

Figure 12.1 – Basic Expert System Model

In step one, an application is selected using guidelines developed to help companies select an appropriate application domain for expert system development. The intent of this step is to find a problem to solve with the technology rather than determine which technology will best fulfill a business need. The existence of this step is symptomatic of expert systems' current imitative and investigative evolutionary stage.

After application selection, the application is defined and project plans are established. In the worst case, some projects have been planned and started with little more definition than "automate whatever it is that Joe does." Because building a knowledge base is an iterative process, project planning often focuses on activities rather than deliverables.

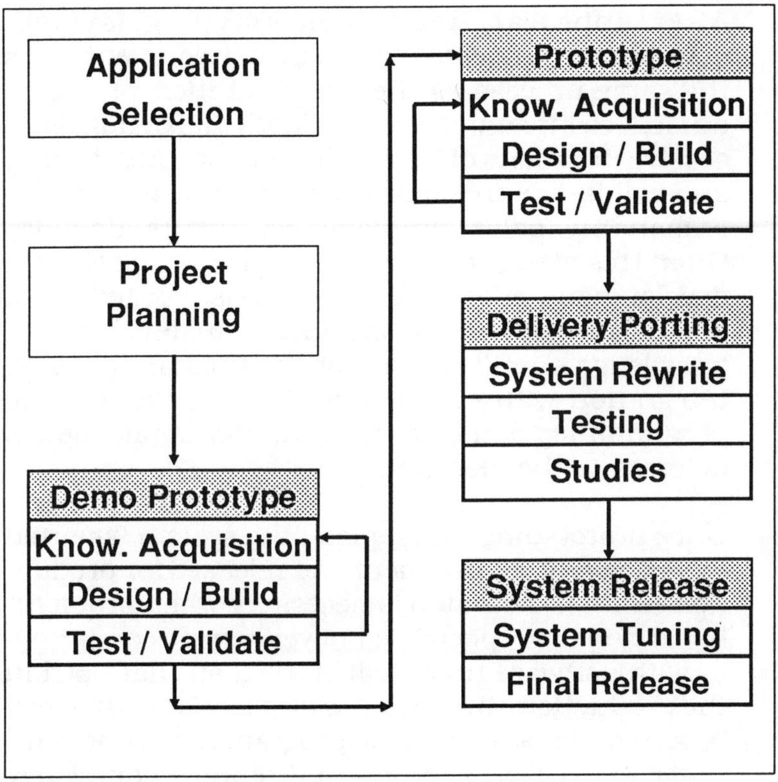

Figure 12.2 – Project Life Cycle - Theory

Next a demonstration prototype is developed which represents 5% to 15% of the final knowledge domain. The many possible reasons for building this prototype are covered in the next chapter; however, the prototype is considered disposable, and is used to obtain approval for the rest of the project. The prototyping process is iterative, so the prototype is continually refined until the project is either scrapped or approved.

After approval, serious prototyping (system development) begins. System development uses the same process as the demonstration prototype but it goes into much greater depth and detail. Successive iterations of knowledge engineering, review, and validation are completed until the system can reasonably solve problems within its domain. Often this step is not considered as a true software development effort. Instead, it is treated as a prototyping process designed to develop the knowledge specification, not the final application. Integration with other computer systems and the programming of the actual computer application is deferred to the next step.

Once prototyping is complete, the system is ported to its delivery environment and released for production testing. This step is necessary when prototyping is done on specialized development computers or with software that is different than that used in the production. In a very few applications, this may be as simple as moving the programs from one computer to another. In others, it entails completely rewriting the prototype into another language so the application can be delivered to end users. Production testing includes a user evaluation period and three studies: system performance, acceptability, and usefulness.

Next, final modifications are made based on the results obtained in production testing, and the system is released to full production.

This development model has been in use for years, and has produced a large number of technically successful demonstration systems, but very few systems that can be considered a business success either because they could not be delivered, or because they were difficult to maintain. Invariably, systems that fail to make it into production never make it out of the prototype stage. The high failure rate is attributable to the following factors:

- The prototype development is seen as the development of technical specifications for the knowledge base rather than the development of the final application.

- Delivery porting is considered trivial; students are typically told that to achieve success over 85% of the total project must be devoted to knowledge engineering.

- Integration, highly efficient user interfaces, multi-user design, testing, and validation are not given the consideration they deserve because expert system technology is viewed as the totality of the solution.

- Development emphasis is placed on demonstrating or discovering technical capability instead of developing basic capabilities that are usable and provide business payback.

- The prototyping process can short-circuit good software design needed to deliver maintainable systems.

Commercial System Model

Commercial applications are most likely to be developed for tasks that are highly paper-oriented and/or people-oriented. In these cases the following conditions are likely to exist.

- The decision makers currently use some combination of paper documents, computer reports, and data inquiry to obtain the information they need for their analysis. When information from paper documents is used, the information is not in the computer system.

- For computer-resident information, applications are probably in use to support inquiry or reporting, but applications to interface with a knowledge base do not exist.

- In many cases, decision makers filter, summarize, and reorganize their information before their analysis begins. Often this is an automatic and instinctive process for humans, but it must be automated by the expert system application. Therefore, existing inquiry and reporting functions may require modification to provide the same function.

- New applications must be built to communicate with the user. These applications may be on-line inquiry and/or batch reports. Either way, the result of the analysis needs to be logically framed and presented to the user or auditor.

Based on these conditions, an integrated, production expert system might look like the one shown in Figure 12.3. The model shown is not intended to be an architectural view of every application; it's only use is to identify potential components that are outlined below.

System Executive

The system executive may not be a single module. One or more modules, or pieces of modules, are required to control the application's operation.

Data Capture

New applications must be built to collect and store information not already computer resident. Existing data collection applications may require modification.

Data Input

Interfaces between new and existing databases and the knowledge server are required to access, filter, and possibly reorganize the data.

User Window

Unless the system is totally autonomous, a user window into the application is required. The window can be any combination of data entry screens, inquiry screens or printed reports. The screens and reports must logically frame and present the results of the knowledge base analysis as well as supporting information and data.

Support

Reporting

In theory, computer systems should cut down on the paper chase. However, paperless applications are extremely rare so it is prudent to expect that a reporting function will be required.

Utilities

At a minimum, facilities are needed to back up and archive data and/or knowledge base results. The utilities may also include test harnesses, a programmer's secret program that can fix anything, or simple job control language for system backups.

Auditing

Auditing is a prudent and necessary part of system administration. Depending on the autonomy and specific application, auditing an expert system application may be more important than it is for conventional systems..

Knowledge Server

The knowledge server is what most refer to as THE expert system. The primary business benefits of the computer application are derived from the knowledge server capability, and the development of the other components would not be necessary without it. The knowledge server includes the knowledge base, inferencing, and knowledge base control structures. Its

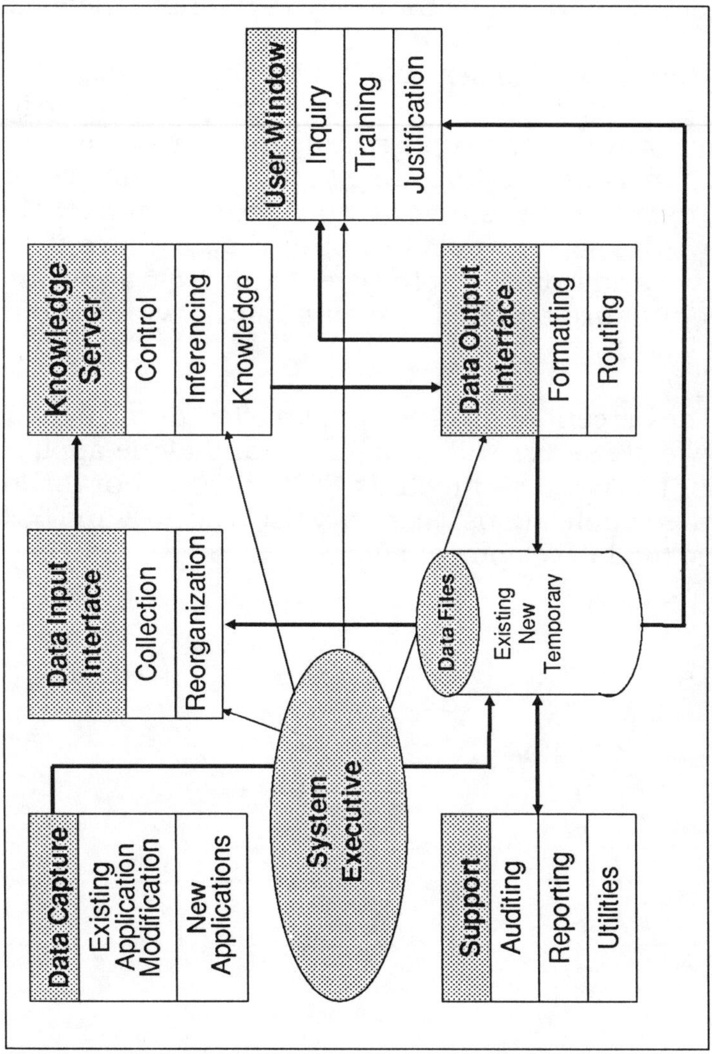

Figure 12.3 – Commercial System Components

purpose is to provide the analysis required, but routing the results of the analysis to the user or other subsystems is handled by the analysis interface modules.

The knowledge server provides the analysis. The conventional software that surrounds the knowledge server provides the support functions for administration, reporting, auditing, integration, and data access. Without these conventional components the knowledge server would be nothing more than a brain in a vat and would lack the eyes, ears, legs, arms, and voice that are required to communicate with the outside world.

The percentage of development effort devoted to the knowledge server will vary – for stand-alone applications it may be as much as 80% to 90%, but for integrated applications it can vary between 25% and 50% of the total development effort.

Commercial Development Model

The development model introduced earlier assumes that prototyping is THE development method, and that all system components are AI related. The development model introduced in Figure 12.4 is almost the opposite; conventional software development techniques dominate, and all system components are first considered conventional until expert system techniques are proven more appropriate. The commercial model is also structured to overcome the problems commonly encountered in expert system development. The model addresses four points of particular concern.

- System capabilities, functions, and features must be clearly understood before development begins. Using only a prototyping approach, the development team feels its way toward the ultimate goal, but cannot clearly define the end result until the prototype is complete.

- Regardless of its power, sophistication, or technical elegance, the expert system will be worthless if users can't or won't use it. Therefore, the mechanics of system delivery are given top priority even at the expense of overlooking some potential benefits that may be discovered in a prototyping process.

- The development approach ties system development, production, and maintenance environments closely together. Without this, a developed system may prove undeliverable, and a delivered system may prove unmaintainable.

- Because knowledge acquisition and knowledge base programming are a discovery process, they are difficult to estimate, but must be tightly controlled and isolated to improve project control and accountability while lowering overall project risk.

It is not the purpose of this book to teach conventional system development methods because there are many excellent books available on the subject. The following discussion is only intended to highlight and emphasize key components. The components discussed are summarized in Figure 12.4.

Project Scope, Goals and Objectives

Confucius has been credited with observing "If you do not know where you are going, any road will take you there." So as a first step, clearly defining the system's scope and objectives is essential. The objectives should be expressed as tangible deliverables in terms of capability, benefits, and usability. Because of the experience-expectation loop, this process will be difficult and imprecise for the first few development projects. However keeping the scope modest, and the objectives reasonable, should be the guiding principle. Surprises, both good and bad, can be expected.

Application Requirements and Specification

Once objectives are established, the application should be completely described and defined from a user perspective. In direct contradiction to the prototyping approach, the output of the system, including reports, screen layouts, wording, and screen movement protocols, should be designed and

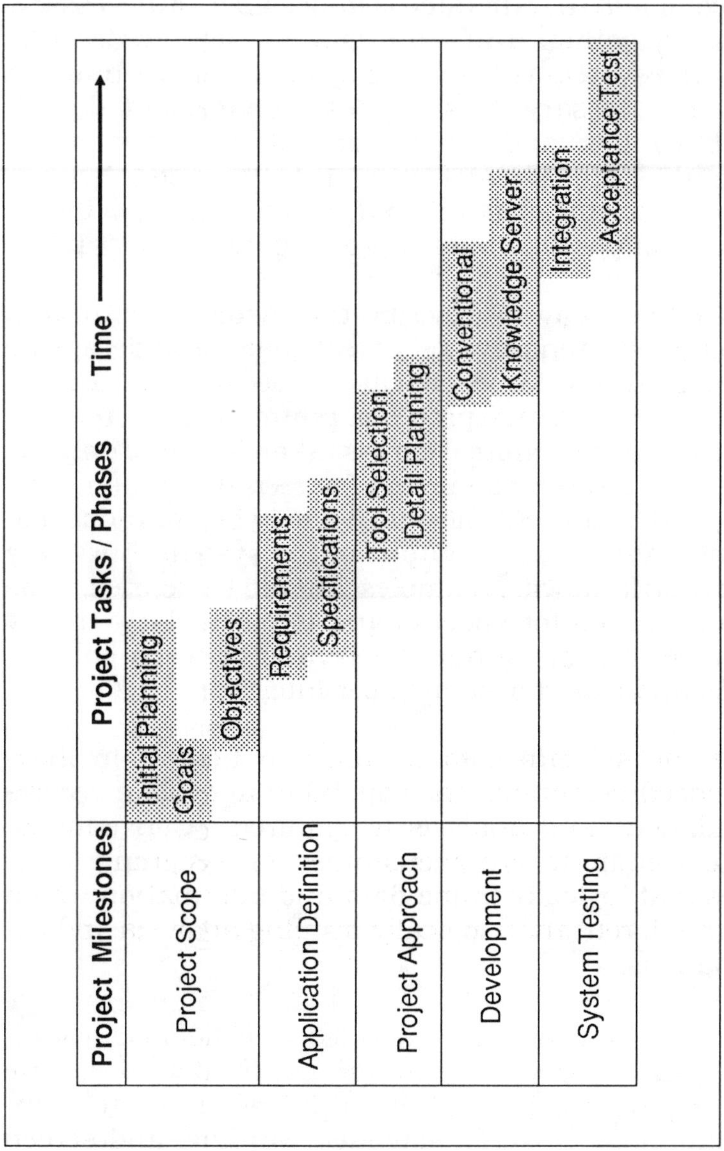

Figure 12.4 – Project Life Cycle – Commercial

described. Proponents of the prototyping approach will complain that this step is impossible, unnecessary, or self-defeating. But – if it is impossible to describe what the system is to do, the system can't be built – if it is unnecessary, this implies management doesn't want to understand what the benefits of the system will be, and – if it is self-defeating, it is because it bounds the project and places it in a business perspective at the cost of possibly missing some potential capability.

The best way to describe the system output is to select a representative set of test cases, and define the system output for each case. Because of the experience-expectation problem, prototyping the user interface may be helpful if care is taken to define only the "look and feel" components of screen navigation, content, and layout. At this stage it may be impractical to define every possible output of the system, but every type of output, with examples, should be defined. This step is crucial for success and is particularly thorny because of some subtle differences between conventional and expert systems user interfaces.

If the system is to be used to help train inexperienced personnel, the capability to explain recommendations and analysis is required. Conventional system analysts are accustomed to designing interfaces that logically frame data and information which is far different than logically framing analysis and explanations.

Professionals usually present their findings in a hierarchical fashion that the user interface may have to replicate. The –

"I conclude . . . because . . . and . . . because . . . ."

used by professionals represents an intertwined network of knowledge, facts, information, and logical reasoning. This places new requirements on the term user-friendly. To be friendly, the screens should support easy user navigation from conclusion to detail data in a way that is logically cohesive.

The situation is entirely different if the system is to be used by experienced personnel; they already know *how*, but they will want to know *why*. The decision process is a discovery process and the explanation facilities normally supplied with expert system development tools explain how the decision was made, but not necessarily why the decision is the most reasonable among other alternatives. The *how* and the *why* processes are not necessarily mirror images of each other. The knowledge base may consider and discard many strategies and facts before the final set of strategies and facts is discovered. Knowledge engineers concentrate on the *how* of the decision which is an assembly process.

For experienced personnel, how the conclusion was reached may no longer be important. Often, a professional can explain hours of thought and analysis in minutes. The *why* explanation can resemble "reverse knowledge engineering," dismantling the conclusion to justify it.

Often a mixture of the two approaches is required. The differences between the two approaches and the benefits of mixing them can be seen in the following dialogue between trainee and teacher.

Teacher: "*What* is your conclusion?"

Trainee: "My conclusion is . . . ."

Teacher: "*Why* do you say that?"

Trainee: "Well, I observed . . . ."

Teacher: "Wait, I think you missed a point. *How* did you arrive at *that* observation – why didn't you consider . . .?"

In order for the prototyping process to be efficient, knowledge engineers usually specify that all information and data available to the expert be made available to the expert system in case it is discovered that it is relevant. Again, the opposite method is proposed – once the output of the system has been specified, the information required to produce the output can be determined by reviewing several test cases with an expert. Limiting the input to the expert system has several benefits: it reduces additional data entry, minimizes interface requirements, and helps establish cost-justification criteria for adding additional functions to the system.

In addition to functional user requirements, engineering specifications such as response time, throughput, number of users, peak processing loads, and target environment should also be defined because they are important for final system acceptance.

Building on the application description and engineering specifications, the system, except for the knowledge server, can be designed. The guiding principle in the design step is to move only those functions appropriate for expert systems to the knowledge server, and keep as much of the system as possible in conventional computer languages.

Project Approach

After the application is understood and designed, the best development strategy, including the development tools, can be determined. This is also a direct contradiction to the popular view that preselects the tool and then looks for a problem to solve. In this approach, the various facets of the problem have been defined, so the best tool to solve each part of the problem can be selected. A mixture of conventional and knowledge base approaches can be expected, but it should not be predestined that an expert system is part of the solution.

How the system will be delivered, tested, and maintained is often overlooked and underestimated in this step. For reasons described later, it is imperative that the system development, production, testing, and maintenance hardware and software environments be identical.

If the need for an expert-system-based solution is determined, most of the project risk and uncertainty will be associated with the knowledge base. To improve project manageability and lower risk, the knowledge base should be isolated from the rest of the project. Treating the knowledge base as a black box with known input and output requirements immunizes conventional component development from risk and uncertainty.

Development

All conventional components of the application should be developed using conventional development methods, while the expert system components should be developed using expert system development methods. Using the definition and the specification of knowledge base inputs and outputs, the knowledge engineering staff will have a clear target and much of the randomness inherent in prototyping will be avoided.

A key consideration in the development cycle is the development of both input and output test harnesses for the knowledge base. The test harnesses are special computer programs that emulate the operation of the data input and data output modules. Rather than working with real data the test harnesses work with test data and provide utilities that help automate knowledge base testing. Expert system development tools are ideal for prototyping, but are remarkably inefficient in file handling and volume testing. Test harnesses are generally unpopular but are beneficial for several reasons:

- Test harnesses use key components of the programs that will provide the necessary integration functions for the system. The test harnesses not only provide test data to the knowledge server, but provide testing for the essential integration software.

13
Prototyping

Prototyping is a valuable systems development technique, but like any other tool it can be misused. In prototyping, rather than develop formal written specifications, users and technical personnel work together to specify, design, and build an application through successive refinement.

Prototyping is an excellent technique to use in application areas that are not well understood, or are ill-defined. Prototyping recognizes that it is often difficult for users and analysts to understand the look, feel, and function of an application from a written specification, but when shown a working prototype they quickly understand. Once users specify changes the prototype is modified and reviewed again. The review/modification process proceeds through several refinement/enhancement iterations until the application is complete. Being tangible, the prototype improves the user-technician communication, and can speed development of high-quality systems tuned to user needs.

Prototyping is an integral part of expert system development, but due to emphasis on ad hoc, stand-alone applications many individuals have accepted it as THE method of development. Prototyping can be used as the singular development technique for small, stand-alone applications, but its value diminishes as application size and level of integration increase.

Prototyping is used in several different ways in expert system development. Some of the ways and their trade-offs are discussed below.

Demonstration Prototypes

Demonstration prototypes, sometimes called *proof-of-concept prototypes*, are the most misused. A demonstration prototype is a scaled down expert system application targeted to handle a few test cases that supposedly represent 5% to 15% of the total knowledge base. Normally built in the system feasibility stage, demonstration prototypes are used to obtain management approval for a full-scale development effort. The emphasis is to rapidly complete the prototype in a few weeks to prove the feasibility of full-scale development as inexpensively as possible. The stated purposes for demonstration prototypes vary but they are usually some variation on the following themes.

To prove to management that the software tools selected can be used to develop a larger-scale, complete application.

To prove to management that the development team is capable of developing expert system applications.

To communicate expert system concepts to management through an actual working model to obtain funding for full system development.

To prove that expert systems are applicable to a particular problem.

The effectiveness of a demonstration prototype depends on how the final application will be used and delivered to end users. For reasons discussed below, demonstration prototypes are more effective for standalone, ad hoc applications, and are least effective for integrated production systems.

The Prototyping Process

Usually two primary constraints placed on demonstration prototype development are time and money. Because of the characteristics of expert system development tools, these constraints force the development team to utilize the user interfaces provided with the development tool, and work around system and file integration issues. However, the most important consequence of the constraints is the severe limitation it places on the size of the knowledge base.

Limiting the prototype to the desired 5% to 15% of the final knowledge base is an impossible objective to achieve or measure. Identifying the desired representative slice of the final knowledge base presupposes the development team understands the knowledge domain. Since the majority of knowledge base development is devoted to knowledge acquisition, this understanding is impossible to achieve in a limited time frame.

Even if the final size of the knowledge base could be estimated, the demonstration prototype would not be able to simulate final system complexity. For example, consider the problem of developing a demonstration prototype for a program designed to play chess.

Theoretically, the prototype should demonstrate system capability, but only represent about 5% to 15% of the knowledge domain. To meet these criteria, one of three approaches can be used: the size of the chess board and the number of pieces can be limited; the parameters of the game can be limited; or only specific examples can be selected for demonstration.

If the size of the board and the number of pieces is limited, one alternative would be to use one-fourth of a full chess board, and only two or three different pieces. Limiting the parameters of the game might include only responding to an opponent's opening move, while demonstrating examples might include eluding a checkmate under constrained circumstances. Since decision complexity tends to grow at least geometrically with the size of the problem, none of the above approaches will provide a valid test. In other words, playing chess on a full chess board is far more complex than playing chess on one-fourth of a board. Because of this, it is unlikely that the limited prototype would represent a reasonable test of the technology, the team, the tools, or the application.

The same is true of most expert systems applications, because developing the first few rules is almost a trivial task, but adding the last, and perhaps the most important, rules can be extremely difficult. In actual practice, development teams usually attempt to develop demonstration prototypes that are either broad-but-shallow, or narrow-but-deep. In the former case, the prototype can handle any extremely simple case. In the latter, the prototype can only handle a few moderately complex cases.

A trap created when a prototype is limited to a few sample test cases is that the test cases become the specification. When this occurs, it is difficult to distinguish good generalized software that happens to handle a few cases from software that has been *hard-wired* to produce the desired answer.

Demonstration Prototype Shortcomings

To bring demonstration prototype shortcomings into focus, each of the four justifications listed in the first section will be reviewed.

- *To prove to management that the software tools selected can be used to develop larger-scale, complete applications.*

  To prove the capability of the software tool, the tool's integration, performance, and technical capabilities should be tested. However, demonstration prototypes seldom attempt to measure these capabilities.

  To meet cost and time constraints, integration is normally ignored and interfaces with existing applications are simulated; therefore no integration test is possible.

  Expert system response times are not a linear function of the size of the knowledge base. Depending on the internal structure of the system, it is likely a one-hundred-rule knowledge base will be more than ten times slower than a ten-rule knowledge base.

The first knowledge collected in expert system development is usually the most basic and simplest to implement. By definition, this is the type of knowledge implemented in a demonstration prototype. Basic knowledge using a few simple rules will not prove the technical capability of the tool to handle the complex inferencing and knowledge strategies that may ultimately be required.

The user interface features provided with most expert system shells work best for ad hoc applications and are not well suited for high-volume production applications. If the application under consideration is a production application, the demonstration prototype will not be able to simulate the final user interface.

The capabilities of the software tools used will not be fully tested with the basic inferencing and knowledge representation strategies employed in the demonstration system.

- *To prove to management that the development team is capable of developing expert system applications.*

Demonstration prototypes fail to provide this test for many of the same reasons mentioned above. Demonstration prototyping does not test the development team's integration, performance tuning, or knowledge engineering skills. Of the three, the knowledge engineering skills are the most important. The farther the team explores the knowledge domain the more complex the problem will become. The situation is analogous to training a bank teller. In a week or two, individuals can be trained in basic procedures to handle most simple transactions. It will take months, however, before they are competent to handle most transactions, and it may take years before they are competent to handle any transaction. Even though the demonstration prototype may represent 5% to 15% of the knowledge domain, it is unlikely it represents 5% to 15% of the effort. For similar reasons, it is unlikely that it will plumb the depths of the tool or the team's technical ability.

- *To communicate expert system concepts to management through an actual working model to obtain funding for full system development.*

It is unlikely that a demonstration prototype can *prove* the benefit of the application, but it may be able to provide examples of the types of processing possible with expert systems. If the examples are basic, as they probably will be, management will still be required to use a measure of imagination to understand the capabilities and benefits of the final application.

- *To prove that expert systems are applicable to a particular problem.*

  Although a demonstration prototype may give some indication of the applicability of expert system technology, it will seldom provide conclusive proof because of the limited scope.

Dangers of Demonstration Prototypes

Using demonstration prototypes to sell expert system concepts can backfire if management does not fully understand their nature and limitations. If the demonstration prototype is oversold, it can lead to unrealistic expectations in the following areas:

The prototype can create unrealistic expectations about the capabilities of the project team and the tools to be used. If the expectations prove invalid, and project problems develop, the technology may be viewed as the culprit, rather than the tools or staff capability.

If the demonstration prototype is too basic, it may appear that there is little difference between expert and conventional systems. This situation occurs most often when conventional programmers try to teach themselves how to build expert systems. There are many examples of these systems, which are little more than a conventional application written in an expert system language. These applications fail to pass the *So what?* test and have unjustifiably devalued the technology.

Some expert system development projects have been aborted in midstream because of unrealistic expectations built on the results of the demonstration prototype. The first of these expectations arises from time estimates. For example, if management is told that a demonstration prototype developed in two weeks represents 10% of the final system, it is reasonable to assume the total project will take twenty weeks. This is almost never the case because of the complexity and integration issues. This problem is magnified when the application under development is a production integrated system. For these applications, experience indicates that over 50% of the total project effort will be devoted to conventional programming, and has nothing to do with the expert system component.

Demonstration Prototype Conclusions

Even though demonstration prototypes are usually abandoned when serious development begins, they can be valuable in educating both technical and nontechnical personnel about the technology and its potential application. Technical personnel become familiar with the development tool and are introduced to the knowledge domain. Users are exposed to the development process and gain some understanding of expert system differences and capabilities. Management personnel benefit by obtaining additional insight into the costs and benefits of the application.

Demonstration prototypes should not be used as a *proof-of-concept* because their results cannot be generalized to full scale development or the final application. If management is not fully aware of the limitations, demonstration prototypes can lead to misunderstandings and total disillusionment about the benefits of expert systems.

If the application is intended to be stand-alone, the demonstration prototype can provide a good model to determine the look and feel of the final system. However, the look and feel of integrated systems can not always be determined from the demonstration prototype. Depending on the level of integration, several levels of software may separate the user and the expert system component. For these types of applications, the user interface may have to be prototyped separately.

Specification Prototypes

If the sole purpose of a demonstration prototype is to help users and managers understand how the proposed application will look, feel, and benefit the organization, time can be better spent developing a specification prototype. A specification prototype is a mock-up of all user screens that permit interscreen navigation and simulate data entry and inquiry.

Specification prototypes examine and help specify *what* the application will do, and avoid getting the *what* of the application confused with the mechanics of *how* the application will operate internally. This is one of the shortcomings of demonstration prototypes since the capability of expert system technology and the way the development team views the technology can influence the user specification. For stand-alone applications, this is unavoidable since many expert system tools bundle the user interface and inference engine in a way that makes it difficult to separate the two.

Specification prototypes are most beneficial when used to define applications that will communicate with the user through conventional software where the knowledge server is only one component in a larger application. Without a specification prototype, determining the best way to frame and navigate through data, information, recommendations, and explanations can be difficult, if not impossible.

Specification prototypes are part of the definition process and help bound the knowledge base by specifying: the necessary depth and breadth of reasoning capability; the necessary and/or available knowledge server inputs; and the required content and structure of knowledge server output. Done properly with the right prototyping tools, the specification prototype does not have to be discarded and can be fleshed-out and extended for use in the production system.

Development Prototypes

Prototyping, an essential element in expert system development, can be used as *the* knowledge acquisition technique, *the* development method, or as a refinement and verification tool.

Knowledge Acquisition

Prototyping is often used as the knowledge acquisition tool. When used this way, the domain expert and the knowledge engineer work together to directly encode rules and knowledge into the system. Each new set of rules is tested, modified, and expanded depending on the results of the test. For small, simple applications, this is totally acceptable, but for larger applications it has serious drawbacks. Just as a carpenter can build a simple bookcase without a blueprint from a general idea, small simple applications can be built using the development prototype as a knowledge acquisition tool. However, it is as unreasonable to expect a carpenter to build a house without a blueprint, as it is to expect a knowledge engineer to build a large system without a good knowledge acquisition plan.

Using the prototype approach as the main knowledge acquisition technique can result in an unstructured, incomplete, and poorly designed knowledge base. This type of knowledge acquisition tends to be random and situational, placing most emphasis on detail (examples) rather than general concepts and rules-of-thumb. If the number of test cases is limited, the knowledge base can take on a structure tailored to solve the test cases and not the general problem domain. The maintainability of the knowledge base can also be adversely affected because the expert and the knowledge engineer may be so bogged down in detail, high-level concepts are missed or incorrectly implemented.

Development Method

Using prototyping techniques as the development method expands the scope of prototyping from just knowledge acquisition to the entire system. This approach suffers from many of the same ills mentioned for knowledge acquisition, and is wholly inappropriate for production, integrated systems. If applicable at all, this method can be used for small stand-alone applications where the development tools are completely self-contained and include inferencing, knowledge base, and user interface capabilities.

In its worst form, this method becomes the definition, design, and development approach all rolled into one, and is guided by only a few vague goals and objectives. This approach suffers from the assumption that expert system technology is a replacement technology and provides little management control over deliverables. Without management control, including clear bounds, objectives, and deliverables, prototyping can quickly degenerate into an exercise to discover what can be done rather than a process to deliver what is needed.

Another danger of prototyping is that systems can grow large, monolithic, and poorly structured with various system components heavily intertwined. In the absence of a detailed set of requirements and a design, prototyping can produce single, large, unmaintainable systems when four or five small systems would have been the most appropriate solution. Before conventional programming design and structuring techniques were developed, many early computer systems exhibited the same "spaghetti code" characteristics. Without a good design and tight control, prototyping is a convenient way to repeat history.

Refinement and Verification

When knowledge acquisition is well planned and structured, prototyping can be used as an effective tool within the context of a larger process. Knowledge base development emphasis is placed on the knowledge acquisition required to deliver the desired capability. Prototyping is used not as the knowledge acquisition or design technique, but as a quality control tool. Once knowledge is acquired, mapped, and verified, it is entered into the system for test and review by the expert. The result of the test can point to knowledge gaps, incorrect knowledge, or misunderstandings. These results become input into the knowledge acquisition process to refine and improve the knowledge acquisition plan. Communication and understanding between the domain expert and the development team are improved, and successive iterations can be completed quickly, but the direction, control, and focus of the development effort is maintained.

14
Testing

The testing and validation of expert systems raise several questions not normally encountered in conventional software. The most formidable question is how to measure the quality of the knowledge base, since its recommendations have both quantitative and qualitative measures. Conventional software testing is binary: the program is right, or it is wrong. The black and white judgment is possible due to the exact specification of the system, which in turn is possible because judgment is not involved, and all experts will agree on the desired outcome.

Applications requiring judgment, interpretation, and analysis are difficult to test for three reasons: The experts will disagree on some of the cases; sometimes there is no right or wrong answer, only answers with varying degrees of desirability; and typically an expert is measured by his ability to produce an acceptable answer most of the time, rather than the best answer all of the time.

Expert systems are based on human knowledge and judgment, and replicate the good along with the bad. Expert systems make mistakes as sure as the system's human counterpart makes mistakes. Because of this, the only valid measure of system performance is relative to the performance of the staff currently doing the analysis. A relative quality standard can be difficult to establish, but the confusion matrix provides a valuable assist.

The Confusion Matrix

The best standard available for expert system measurement is the past performance of human decision makers. If the purpose of the system is to improve the quality and consistency of the decisions made by the professional staff, then the system has to be able to perform better than the average employee. To measure this performance, a representative set of test cases and a scoring mechanism are required.

The test cases should be real cases handled in the normal course of business with the decision/recommendation made at that time. The cases should be real, because nothing is as strange as reality, and try as we may, we rarely can create realistic test cases. Initially, the cases should not be reanalyzed to check the original decision, because the analyst will use extra care and caution once he knows the decision will be open to scrutiny.

The scoring mechanism is the confusion matrix which has two input components. To construct the first component, all of the possible outcomes have to be listed and rated by the cost of confusing one outcome with another.

For example, assume that a stock advisor system is to be measured against the performance of a group of portfolio managers. For simplicity, assume the system can make only one of four recommendations: buy, sell, hold, or reevaluate in one hour. These four recommendations make up the first component in the confusion matrix as shown in Figure 14.1, which lists *the* best recommendation horizontally, and the actual recommendation vertically. The next step is to rate the cost of confusing the actual recommendation with the best recommendation.

For purposes of this example, assume that the worst possible situation would be to recommend a buy position when the best decision would be to sell. Also assume that on average whenever this situation occurred it cost the investment house $1000. In a similar fashion, all other possible combinations are rated based on their actual average cost.

Figure 14.1 shows a completed table using average costs. Any cost index can be used provided it is consistent and shows the relative cost between the worst

Figure 14.1 – Relative Cost of Confusion

	Best Recommendation			
Actual Decision	**Buy**	**Sell**	**Hold**	**Reevaluate**
Buy	0	1000	500	400
Sell	750	0	400	400
Hold	350	500	0	50
Reevaluate	100	100	20	0

and best cases. Using cost indices is a negative measure, but positive measures can be used to show the benefits of one decision over another.

Completing the second table requires that the test cases be carefully reviewed to determine the best solution, and categorize the past recommendations. If one hundred test cases were used, the second table might appear as shown in Figure 14.2. The table plots the number of times each recommendation was made against what would have been the *best* recommendation. Finally, a numeric rating is computed for actual performance by multiplying corresponding values in the tables shown in Figures 14.1 and 14.2 and totalling the results as shown in Figure 14.3.

The tricky step in this process is determining what would be the best answer. The best answer can be determined by a single expert, or by a consensus of several experts on cases where there could be differences of opinion. In this step, the identity of the

Figure 14.2 – Number of Decisions – Actual vs Best

	Best Recommendation			
Actual Decision	**Buy**	**Sell**	**Hold**	**Reevaluate**
Buy	18	1	1	1
Sell	1	22	1	1
Hold	1	1	25	4
Reevaluate	3	3	4	13

original decision maker, the decision made, and the outcome of the decision should not be known to the expert(s) to avoid a subconscious skewing of the analysis. Using this approach, the standard developed should be higher than the normal performance of even the experts, because their analysis will be more critical and thorough than would be possible during normal day-to-day work. This additional analysis may be very labor intensive, but it is necessary for development and testing, and it does define a standard that is the best the organization can possibly do.

Theoretically, the best possible level of performance is defined as a numerical rating of zero. Actual performance in this example is rated at 5,180. The worst possible level of performance, *i.e.* making the worst possible recommendation in every case, would result in a numerical rating of 62,350. However, actual per-

Figure 14.3 – Total Confusion Cost – Cost Times Frequency

	Best Recommendation			
Actual Decision	**Buy**	**Sell**	**Hold**	**Reevaluate**
Buy	0	1000	500	400
Sell	750	0	400	400
Hold	350	500	0	200
Reevaluate	300	300	80	0
Col. Totals	1400	1800	980	1000
Grand Total	5180			

formance should not be measured against this number because pure random distribution would result in a numerical rating of 28,560. This method measures not only quantity (the original recommendations were right 87% of the time), but quality (how good the recommendations were in the remaining 13%). Because of the two measures, actual performance on the test cases would be rated at 81.9% since 5,180 is 18.1% of 28,560.

Once an actual performance benchmark is established, measuring the performance of the system is accomplished by plotting the system's recommendations and calculating its numerical rating. As will be discussed in the chapter on cost justification, this method can be used to determine what level of performance the system must achieve to be cost justified, and that level can be used as the minimum acceptable performance level for testing, certification, and system acceptance.

Development, Delivery, and Maintenance

The best way to insure a quality system that is easy to maintain and use is to consider the delivery and maintenance as the first development issues rather than the last.

A carryover from years past when integration and delivery were minor concerns, the use of development prototypes as the knowledge acquisition tool reinforces the belief that the prototype and the final system are two distinct entities. For knowledge acquisition prototyping to be effective, the development tool must be very facile and responsive. The development tools best suited for knowledge acquisition may not be the best for production use. The result is two distinct systems, a production system and the prototype, each written in different languages or dialects, and operating in different environments.

Since knowledge acquisition is the most difficult task, it is argued that once the knowledge acquisition is complete everything else is trivial. This school of thought teaches it is acceptable to rewrite the prototype into another language to get the system delivered. This "means justifies the end" approach has four problems.

First, once the knowledge acquisition prototype is complete, it must be completely tested. Testing the prototype can be extremely difficult because many development tools are exclusively dedicated to dialogue-intensive user interfaces, and have limited file integration capability. Without the ability to automatically load and run test cases, intensive and extensive testing is very costly. Manual testing can be so error prone, time consuming, and labor intensive some companies have been trapped into releasing a prototype for production conversion based on results obtained from less than ten test cases.

Second, it is unlikely that two different tools used for development and delivery have identical knowledge representation and rule structures. The system, once translated, must be retested just to prove that the translation was done properly. After the translation has been verified, intensive production testing must be completed. Production testing will produce changes to both rules and knowledge structures to fix errors, close knowledge gaps, and improve system response time.

As these inevitable changes are made the production system will begin to look less and less like the prototype.

Third, since the prototyping tool was justified for its knowledge acquisition assistance, it will certainly be justified as a knowledge acquisition tool for maintenance and enhancement. However the result will be double maintenance and double testing on two different systems that supposedly do the same thing, but in different ways, languages, and environments. It takes a tremendous leap in faith to believe this method is effective, efficient, and capable of being audited.

Fourth, this approach defers important interface and integration development and testing to the end of the project, increasing overall project risk. Most production applications will fail, regardless of the knowledge base quality, if these problems are not solved. If integration is a prerequisite, it should be resolved first, not last. Project risk is also increased by deferring the translation effort, performance tuning, and testing.

If the proposed development prototype is in any way different than the delivery system, the approach should be carefully considered. It may be better to use one tool for development and delivery even if it suboptimizes knowledge acquisition. The single tool approach eliminates a system rewrite and a great deal of duplicate work. It also allows performance tuning and integration development to proceed as an integral part of the overall development process rather than as an add-on at the end of the project.

Testing

Testing is as important for expert systems as it is for any software system. The amount and type of testing varies depending on the application's size, use, and level of autonomy. The method of testing varies but the same basic principles apply.

The Testing Problem

Certainty, error identification, and quality measurement are the three key testing problems with knowledge systems.

Testing certainty measures the level of confidence in the system that can be established from the testing program. By using structured testing methodologies on conventional software, every logic path through the system can be tested and verified. Structured testing leads to high confidence in the quality of the system. However, the number of logic paths through a knowledge base system can be quite large, and it may be unreasonable to even attempt to identify all of them.

The solution is a combination of technical and user-level testing. Knowledge engineers can test individual rules or rule sets to technically verify the rules are producing the desired results. User-level testing represents integration testing at the knowledge base level and verifies, within reasonable limits, the operation of the system.

The confusion matrix provides a method of identifying errors and measuring quality, however error identification needs further discussion. Using the confusion matrix, an error is defined as making a recommendation different than that identified by the expert as being the best. A common occurrence in expert system application is that the expert proclaims the system as being capable of outperforming him. Since the best the expert can do is defined as a zero confusion matrix rating, how can this be?

Although knowledge acquisition requires the use of one governing expert, the knowledge of multiple experts and/or specialists can be captured and used by the system. The knowledge acquisition process is also a learning experience for the experts because every facet and nuance of their knowledge and decision process will be explored, examined, questioned, and possibly improved upon. As a result, the knowledge acquisition process usually results in improving the definition of *the best*, and the confusion matrix standard requires continual adjustment.

Running Test Cases

The number of factors management must consider in determining how and to what extent to test an expert system is enormous. Some applications may require rigorous testing while others may be successful with simple, informal testing. What follows is a discussion of testing for large critical applications. It is left to the reader to scale this approach back to fit each particular situation or devise other methods.

Test Harnesses

Expert system development tools are primarily designed to develop interactive applications. This can present a testing obstacle even if a small number of test cases are to be used. If each test case must be entered manually, extensive testing will become very labor intensive and will require an additional level of verification to identify data entry errors. Manual testing has management implications, since a natural tendency of development and maintenance personnel is to trim testing when under deadline pressures.

For large integrated production systems it becomes easy to justify test harnesses that can automatically run test cases for verification. Use of test harnesses will improve the effectiveness of knowledge engineering personnel in two ways. First, they will have a comprehensive, stable test suite for the system to help identify errors, close knowledge gaps, and tune the knowledge base to improve response time. Second, since test cases are entered, verified, and stored once and do not have to be reentered for every test, knowledge engineering personnel can spend more time developing and less time testing.

Once development is complete, the test harness can become the test vehicle for maintenance personnel to verify changes are producing the desired results and have not introduced new errors.

User Testing

User testing refers to testing to insure the application is meeting reasonable development, quality, and functional objectives. The testing methods advocated here do not require users to actually test the system at each level; some of the testing will be done by the knowledge engineering staff. The user testing methods presented can be applied to small or large systems, and can be applied to demo prototypes, development prototypes, and production systems.

The objective of the testing regime is to verify the application can handle real cases, within quality limits. Management can usually identify the number of test cases required to provide a test sample that reasonably models the characteristics of the application's case load. The best way to develop test cases is to select them from actual cases that have been handled in the past. For reasons that will be discussed below, the number of test cases selected should be four times the number identified by management as a reasonable test sample. Once the test cases have been selected, they should be randomly split into four groups to be used as follows:

- Knowledge Base Development
- Knowledge Base Internal Testing
- Knowledge Base Acceptance Testing
- Knowledge Base Certification

Initially, only the first set of test cases should be provided to the development team. The last three sets should be used in blind testing where the development team has no knowledge of their contents. This is prudent to guard against the subconscious tendency of the development team, including the domain expert, to tailor knowledge to the test set.

The first set of test cases is provided to the development team as a development tool. By using the confusion matrix, the development team can use this set as an objective measure of the knowledge base development. The test set can also be used to establish project milestones by stating the percentage of the test cases that will be correctly handled by a particular date. By default, the test set also identifies the depth and breadth of knowledge required by the final system, so development continues until the system meets the desired quality standard.

Once the quality standard is reached, the second set of test cases is entered and run against the system. The knowledge base internal testing performs several important functions. First, as a blind test, it verifies the general structure and design of the knowledge base, and can be used to prove the system was not designed just to handle the development cases. Second, it will inevitably identify a few problem areas, either bugs or knowledge gaps that require resolution. Problem correction should continue until the system meets or exceeds the quality standard for the composite test suite.

Users become involved in the third phase, User Acceptance Testing. This is another blind test, and if the development team has done a good job only a few minor problems should occur. At this stage, a few changes may be required to accommodate user needs and, as in earlier tests, testing should continue until acceptable quality standards are achieved.

The fourth and final test, System Certification, is a hands-off test. If the system is ready for production, the fourth set of test cases can be added to the previous three and the total run against the system without quality degradation. If this occurs, the system can be put into use with reasonable confidence. Another measure of confidence can also be achieved by plotting the trend in confusion matrix ratings between the different tests. As long as the trend line is level or improving, it indicates a complete, high-quality system.

Maintenance

All software follows the same life cycle. Systems will be in a maintenance mode most of their lives, and maintenance costs can far exceed the initial cost of development. Expert systems are roughly following the same evolutionary path traversed by conventional software. Once the capability of conventional software was discovered, delivery became an issue. To improve deliverability, third generation languages replaced Assembler language. As the number of delivered applications grew, the maintenance backlog began to grow even faster. Development productivity had been improved, but systems needed to be maintainable so structured design and software engineering techniques became an essential part of system development.

The maintenance problem with expert systems is more acute than it is with conventional software. Conventional software maintenance is "on demand" to fix errors or extend capability. Expert system software maintenance must be continuous since knowledge is continuously changing and expanding. Expert systems are in the delivery phase of their evolution, maintainability has yet to be discovered or addressed.

Since proven design standards that improve maintainability have not emerged, companies must do the best they can and look for ways to lower maintenance risks.

Besides thoughtful design, keeping knowledge bases small and modular and providing a comprehensive test environment are the most prudent development approaches. Even after the proven design standards have emerged, measuring the impact of enhancements and regression testing will be necessary. As such, investing the time to build test harnesses, establish objective test criteria, and develop realistic test cases will be developmental necessities.

15

Development Strategies

Project Control

Testing performance and capability against an objective standard is an essential project control tool for expert system development. There are numerous objective measures that can be employed in conventional software development: Specifications can be reviewed and signed off; modules can be counted and checked off when complete; and subsystems can be identified, and tested for completeness and accuracy. Unfortunately there is no way to internally quantify and estimate knowledge base intangibles such as reasoning ability, depth of knowledge, breadth of knowledge, and quality of knowledge. For a project manager to know where his project stands, external measures are required, and again the confusion matrix can be employed.

The previous discussion on testing looked at only the final result or the final recommendation, but most systems of reasonable size contain multiple knowledge bases, subject areas, and levels of recommendations. When a prototyping approach is used and guided by the "automate Joe" project goal the result is likely to be a large tangled knowledge base that attempts to automate an entire process rather than just key decision/analysis functions within the process.

In such cases, the expert system is placed in control of a process (read *procedure*). Since expert system technology is inherently nonprocedural, this is a fundamental design error that will drive up development and maintenance costs. Use conventional software to drive procedures and processes – use expert systems software to drive analysis.

It may have taken Joe seven or more years to become the company expert. If the project attempts to automate the totality of Joe's experience, more sophisticated software and advanced knowledge engineering and acquisition techniques will be required. If we remember the relationship between length of experience and development tools and techniques, a better approach would be to divide Joe's job into several pieces, each of which require one year's experience to achieve competence.

So rather than implementing single large systems, the guiding principle should be to divide and conquer by breaking the problem into smaller components each of which is deliverable and testable. For example, a system designed to help in order entry and approval may have several logical components.

- Order Review For Completeness and Consistency
- Credit Approval
- Identification of Order Subcomponents
- Subcomponent Ordering and Scheduling
- Order Assembly Specification
- Order Packaging and Shipping
- Order Entry Into the Computer System

This particular order entry application does not represent a single task, but multiple tasks in a process. Depending on other characteristics of the application, each of the seven tasks would be implemented as individual knowledge bases or as separate expert systems.

Each task would require knowledge about several different subject areas, and the system could be designed to handle some tasks automatically. For example, the system might automatically prepare forms necessary to complete missing information, advise the user of inconsistencies, automatically approve credit for standard cases, and refer questionable credit risks to the user with analysis and recommendations.

Each task and task subcomponent represents a decision or recommendation that requires testing. If system design is functional, as it should be, development and delivery of each function can be isolated, tested, and signed off using the confusion matrix. Breaking the order process into small tasks improves system reliability and maintainability as well as providing a method of building quality into the final system.

The 80/20 Rule

Expert system projects are notorious for ever-expanding knowledge bases, functional requirements, and project budgets. To maintain control over development projects, scope and objectives must be clearly defined from the outset. The 80/20 rule can be used to help set objectives and priorities for development projects as well as define a logical growth path for the system over time. A restatement of the law of diminishing returns, the 80/20 rules states that 80% of the system's benefit is derived from 20% of the project cost, and 80% of the cost is attributable to only 20% of the benefits. In any project the actual percentages vary, but the rule reminds us that most projects can be organized to work on high-yield problems first.

Application of the 80/20 rule, in addition to assisting project management, produces positive ripple effects by delivering benefits earlier, lowering development costs, and reducing staff costs. Use of the 80/20 rule only requires that an organization understand what it is trying to accomplish with the system, and what problem or opportunity the system is to address. Most potential applications can be analyzed in a manner similar to the confusion matrix and plotted as a bar graph similar to Figure 15.1.

Figure 15.1 graphically displays the cost of a particular error multiplied by its frequency. The same analysis can be applied to the benefits associated with capitalizing on opportunities, alternative decisions within the same decision domain, or subdecisions in processes such as underwriting or credit analysis. However the method is applied, the purpose is to identify the largest target of opportunity and zero-in on the largest payback first.

Prototyping tends to be nondiscriminate, and development of a system using this technique will usually result in a benefit return similar to that shown in Figure 15.2 where some improvement is gained in all areas. However, some of the areas may not be worth

Figure 15.1 – Total Error Cost by Type of Error

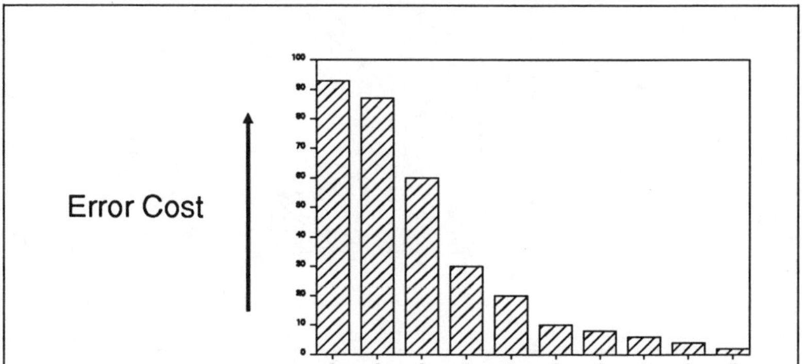

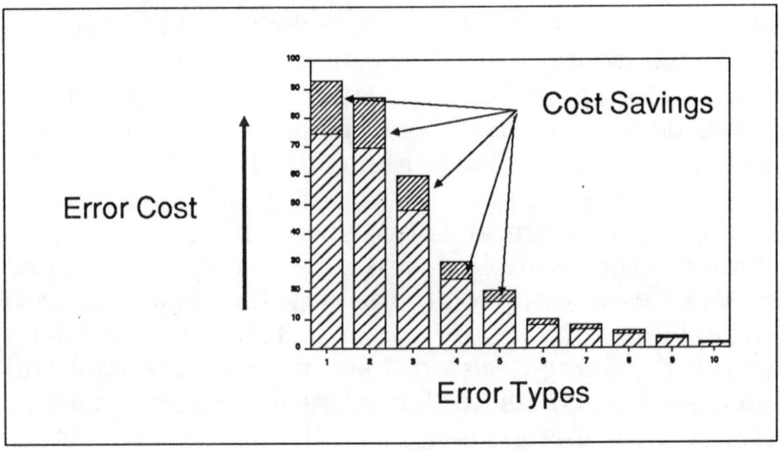

Figure 15.2 – Uniform Quality Improvement

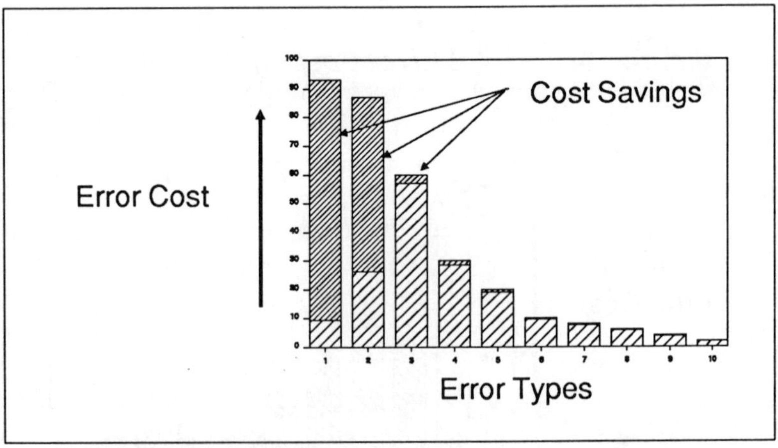

Figure 15.3 – Targeted Quality Improvement

worrying about from a cost-benefit standpoint. Expert systems are like conventional systems: Programming for exception and rare case handling can consume the lion's share of the development budget.

Given a properly guided development effort, a lessor or equivalent amount of effort could produce a benefit return similar to that shown in Figure 15.3. Taking this approach the major targets of opportunity are addressed first and a clear next step for system growth is established. Even though only the first two areas were addressed, some benefit is likely to accrue to the other problem areas by default due to improved training, improved productivity, or professional effectiveness. Other positive cost-containment ripple effects can be expected since the amount of development effort can grow nonlinearly with increased reporting, auditing, data entry, file transfer, and knowledge base requirements.

Rabbit Hunting

Another aspect of maintaining a narrow focus is that it permits a company to use smaller, less costly tools. A common occurrence, especially among large companies, is to assume that their applications will require the most powerful and sophisticated tools, so they begin development at that level. This approach completely ignores the possibility that the application may not require a high level of tool power and staff sophistication. The reverse strategy, rabbit hunting, assumes that, until proven otherwise, every application is a candidate for small tool implementation. If the small tool cannot solve the problem, the large tool, the elephant gun, is brought into play.

This approach has several virtues, especially when combined with the 80/20 rule and the divide and conquer principle. Applications that outwardly appear to be large, complex, and proper candidates for large tool development are broken up into smaller pieces that are easier to build/maintain and deliver in increments. In the large tool approach, it is not uncommon for development to deliver single monolithic solutions instead of smaller building blocks. The worst that can happen using the rabbit hunting approach is that the tool proves inadequate for the problem domain. However, the time spent in knowledge acquisition and knowledge base development is not lost and is mostly recoverable as domain familiarization and specification. Once the team switches to the larger tool they will have done much of the knowledge acquisition and will have a better understanding of the problem.

Knowledge Acquisition

Another benefit of keeping things small relates back to competence and knowledge acquisition skills. It may take years for an individual to become competent in all aspects of a particular task. However, when the task is subdivided into subject or decision areas, each area will take less time to achieve a high level of competence.

Even with simple knowledge domains, some training and education should be provided to the development staff for knowledge acquisition and engineering so the developer can eclectically select those techniques that produce the best results. Knowledge acquisition and system analysis techniques are tools designed for handling problems of different complexity.

To universally apply the highly formal and sophisticated knowledge acquisition techniques to every application just because it is an expert system project does not make business sense.

Typical Growth Patterns

To use expert system technology, a company's user and technical staffs must first learn and internalize the technology just as they would with any other technology such as relational data bases. A typical pattern is emerging that companies are using to internalize expert system technology.

The first phase of internalization is the technology transfer phase during which a company moves from the observer category into actual prototype development. In the usual mode, a company will utilize PC shells to develop small demonstration systems for evaluation. The demonstration systems, after evaluation, are ultimately developed into full-size, standalone applications for one or more users. Often, in this phase there is a preoccupation with analysis, evaluation, and development of toy applications. Those companies that show good forward progress avoid toy applications. Instead they pick real, but small, applications that will provide benefit for their first development efforts. Once companies have a few small successes, they face their first big hurdle – expansion of scope.

In the second phase, the size and scope of applications are increased forcing additional attention on integration and production interfaces. Most expert system failures occur during the second phase. The failures are not technical; the prototypes produce acceptable results, but are incapable of being ported into a production environment. The failures in this phase are caused by a multitude of factors that all boil down to a preoccupation with technology, overuse of prototyping, and a lack of definition that fails to encompass the final production and maintenance problems.

The third and final phase, rollout, is by far the most difficult for a company to complete. In this phase, a company must solve the many technical issues of integration as the first production systems are deployed.

The three phases represent the typical company pattern and roughly correspond to the research pattern of propose, research/prove, and then apply. The first phase is a good first step provided management sets specific objectives and benefits to be achieved. The last two phases are an artifact of the heritage and beliefs in the AI community and should be handled as a single integrated phase. There is no use in building a prototype unless questions about integration and production use are answered first.

Challenges

Selling The Technology

The first challenge an expert system champion faces is in selling the technology to management. Often this is a chicken-and-the-egg problem. Until management can see and understand the benefits, there is no budget. Without a budget, the time and money required to convince management does not exist.

Demonstration prototypes are often used as a low-cost, low-risk means of selling management on the technology. However, management does not buy technology; it buys answers to problems or access to opportunities. So in "selling the technology," don't – sell a solution. If there is a problem worth solving, the technology is secondary and sells itself. If the problem isn't worth solving, the most wondrous technology won't help make the sale.

Integration

The capabilities of vendor-supplied development tools are rapidly changing for the better. As the technology matures less emphasis is being placed on demonstrating capability and emphasis is now shifting to delivering business benefit. Because of this shift, the new buzzword in the industry is integration and many vendors now claim compatibility with IBM computer systems. Despite the apparent compatibility, buyers are encouraged to read the fine print because there are three levels of compatibility – hardware, communication, and environment.

The first level of compatibility is strictly at the hardware level. Hardware compatibility is achieved when a tool can be used on a given computer. Because of the availability of cross-compilers, translators, and emulators, this level of compatibility is relatively easy to achieve, but it does not necessarily mean the development tool can be used effectively.

To be used effectively, the tool and the programs developed using the tool must be able to communicate with other software on the same computer. This must be a two-way communication path. Conventional computer programs should be able to communicate with and control the expert system and the expert system should be able to communicate with and control conventional programs. For development tools originally designed for use on LISP computers, this is a much more difficult level of compatibility to achieve.

Even with hardware and communication compatibility, a development tool may be totally useless if it is hostile to its intended operating environment. To achieve environmental compatibility, software must be a good computer citizen and behave according to normal software engineering rules. An expert system that takes up one third of the computer's available memory, is not multi-user, uses too much computer time, or violates operating system standards is not computer-friendly and will probably never be placed into production.

16
Cost Justification

This chapter is divided into three sections. The first two sections present a thumbnail sketch of the costs and benefits. These two sections bring together concepts introduced and developed elsewhere. The last section deals with application justification.

The following discussion presents a quick outline for cost-benefit analysis that is neither application nor company specific. What follows is only one of several possible models and will require modification before it can be applied to a specific application or company. It is also independent of application type and deployment method. In any particular situation, components may have to be added or deleted. What follows is not absolute, it is a guide.

Costs

Depending on a company's situation, four key cost elements should be considered. The first two elements, development and maintenance costs, are fairly standard. Additionally, if a company does not have an expert system capability, start-up costs, which include staffing and environmental costs, must be considered.

The cost of developing an expert system application has traditional and expert system components. The major cost categories are environment, staff, application development, and application maintenance as shown in Figure 16.1.

Environment

Environmental costs are usually easy to identify and are outlined in Figure 16.2. Environmental costs include hardware and software costs associated with the expert system. If the application is to be developed and delivered on the company's current computer, hardware costs will generally not be an issue. Personal computer applications or applications designed for specialized hardware may require the purchase of additional hardware to support the development or to deliver the application.

On the software side, the development tools must be licensed. Care should be exercised in costing the software component for two reasons. First, many of

Figure 16.1 – Application Cost Components

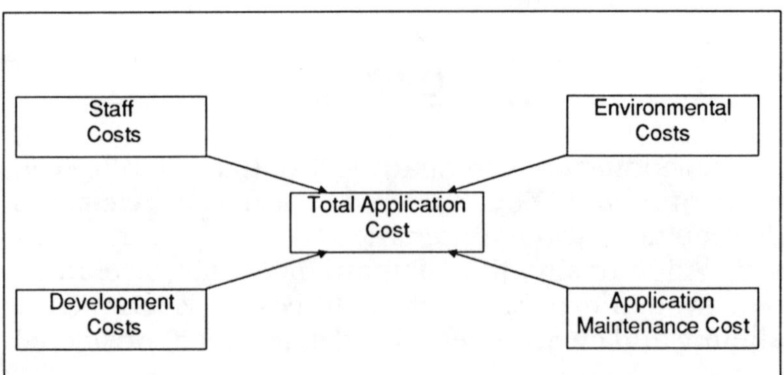

the expert system development tools are licensed on a per computer or a per user basis and may or may not require special additional licensing before the system is delivered to end users. Second, before starting the project thorough research should be completed to identify all of the licensed software that will be needed for development and delivery. It is important not to hamstring the development team by overlooking the software that will be required to handle control, communication, data access, and interface functions. Depending on the development tool selected, a separate software package may need to be licenced to handle each of these functions. These items may appear to be expensive at the outset, but without them the development team will waste valuable time working around the limitations of the expert system development tool to provide these procedural functions.

Figure 16.2 – Environmental Cost Components

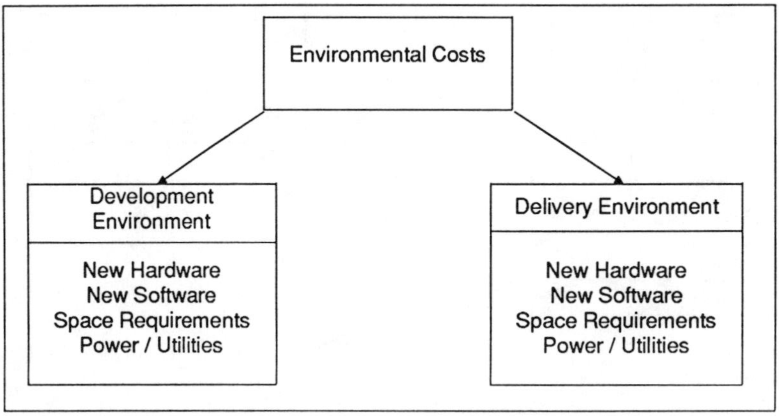

Staff

The development tool selected is the single largest factor in determining staff costs. The more sophisticated the development tool, the scarcer the skills and the more training required. Staffing costs are also affected by corporate goals and objectives and current staff depth/availability as depicted in the Figure 16.3..

The single largest problem companies face is acquiring the prerequisite skills to begin development of any type. Software and hardware, if required, are readily available, but experienced personnel are rare and are generally concentrated in narrow pockets along the east and west coasts. Due to the skill shortage, companies wishing to build expert system applications have to be creative in the way they build

Figure 16.3 – Staff Cost Components

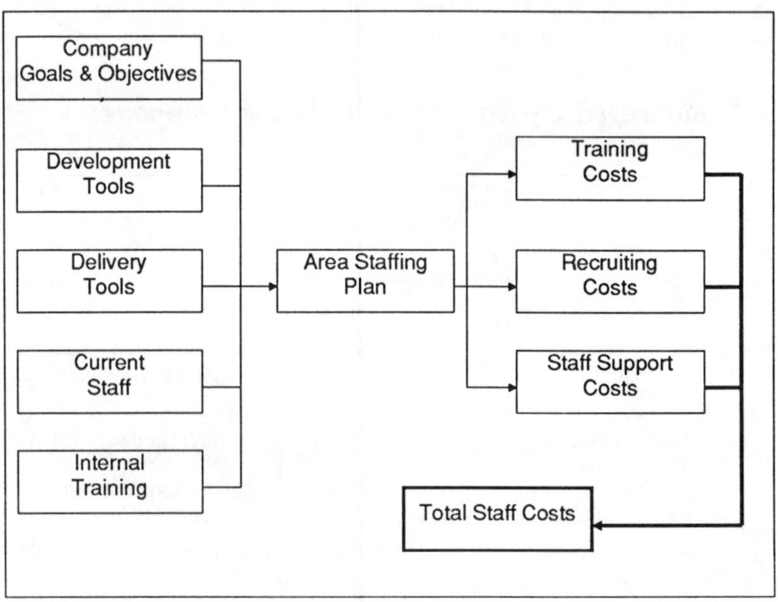

their internal staffs. Several alternatives are discussed below and can be mixed and matched to create hybrid staffing strategies.

Although this section concentrates on knowledge engineering skills, it does not imply that only knowledge engineering skills are required. Most useful applications require a balanced development team that possesses both conventional and expert system skills.

Recruiting

The first, and perhaps most obvious, approach is to contact placement firms specializing in knowledge engineers, and continue to hire from the outside until a staff of sufficient size has been recruited. Almost any AI vendor has contacts or knows of placement firms that specialize in knowledge engineers. They are generally willing to help any prospective customer and may even be able to provide the names of several candidates.

This method, while being the most direct, is probably the most expensive and risky. Any time a new employee is hired there is a risk that the new employee will not work out. This situation is especially acute in the knowledge engineering market because of the high salaries and the placement fees that are based on annual compensation. One of the other drawbacks is the new employee may know expert systems, but will face a substantial learning curve before he becomes familiar with your business and company policies. If the new employee comes from a research or technical background, employers also run the risk that the new employee may not have the balanced perspective and training required to build business systems. Before taking the recruiting route, it is well worth the effort to locate a copy of AI Magazine, the official publication of the American Association for Artificial Intelligence (AAAI), and review the help wanted ads. The ads will provide information on key motivator, orientation, and background requirements for knowledge engineers.

As an alternative, a modified recruiting approach can be utilized to hire only the lead knowledge engineer, and allow him/her to determine the best staffing strategies for the remainder of the staff.

Technology Transfer

Another popular strategy is to hire consultants or vendor personnel to help develop the first few applications and train an internal staff in the process. This method, when combined with outside training classes in knowledge engineering and knowledge acquisition, can work very well. However, there are two important points to consider. First, different training classes in the same subject should be used when possible so staff members can obtain different perspectives. Second, the consultant should be hired to train, not build the application.

The second point is the most crucial and the one most often missed. Consultants, by their nature, want to do as much of the project as you will allow. The more they do, the more they earn, the better their resumes – but the less your staff learns. You can't learn to ride a bicycle by watching someone else, nor can you learn with training wheels. The only way to learn is by doing, preferably under the guidance of a teacher, and with the expectation of several small failures before success is achieved.

If the goal of the project is to get an application into production as fast as possible, it makes sense to let the consultants build the system. If the goal of the project is to deliver a system and train a staff, hire the consultant as a teacher and/or project leader. If the consultant builds the system without training the staff, a company can find itself in an untenable position, with a system in production and no way to maintain or enhance it without relying on the consultant.

Using consultants as teachers can be a very effective strategy because they have to spend less time learning your business, and the amount of time they spend on the project should diminish as the project progresses.

Universities

A slight variation on the consultant strategy is to use local universities. Most universities now offer courses in expert systems and welcome the opportunity to work with companies on a project or two. Most university professors are eager for practical experience and a little extra income. Their rates tend to be lower than professional consultants, they are qualified and effective educators, they are less likely to have a specific vendor bias, and their orientation is to help their students grow to independence.

University Recruiting

As a side note on the university strategy, some companies have contracted with universities to have their first prototype built by either graduate or undergraduate students as part of their class assignment. This approach can be an ideal situation for all involved. The students and university get practical experience; the company gets a low-cost, low-risk evaluation; the university makes a little money; and the company gets recognition as a good corporate citizen by helping fund the local university. Usually in the process, the company and the students get introduced and the company now has a leg up in recruiting the better students who are already familiar with the company.

Recruiting college graduates also has another advantage. Once a programmer has several years of conventional programming background, it often takes several months to untrain him/her before the real expert systems training can begin. College graduates have the conventional training, but do not require deprogramming to be effective knowledge engineers. Some rather large expert systems have been built almost totally by recent college graduates given proper guidance and some additional education.

Internal Cross Training

A final method of developing internal capability is to cross train existing programmers. This approach is time consuming and should be combined with both active and passive training. Passive training includes outside courses, while active training is on-the-job training. The active training should be supervised by an experienced knowledge engineer if it is to be completed in a reasonable length of time. We can learn how to play chess by reading a book, but we do not develop chess-playing skill until we begin to play against a skilled opponent. The same is true for expert systems. We may learn and develop skills over time without someone of experience helping us, but it will take a great deal of time and effort.

Staff cross training should be an integral part of any staffing strategy because it broadens the depth of the development organization. Existing employees already know the business and can help expert system projects leverage the richness most organizations have in their current computer systems.

When cross training is considered, look beyond the technical staff to find knowledge workers in your organization. If you think of the work teachers perform – mine, organize, filter, and feed back knowledge – it is very similar to what a knowledge engineer must do. In general, the skills and traits that make for a good teacher are the same that make for a good knowledge engineer.

Application Development

Application development costs include application definition, specification, programming, and testing. Each of these three development components should be divided into three elements: knowledge base development, conventional software development, and training/documentation.

Standard system development estimating procedures result in reasonable estimates for conventional program development as well as documentation and training. Lack of experience and knowledge uncertainty makes estimating the knowledge base component less precise and cost estimates should reflect this.

Items most often overlooked in estimating development cost are: time to develop and analyze test cases, time to build test harnesses, and staff time for the system expert and users.

Maintenance Costs

Need triggers conventional software maintenance and enhancement. An expert system is like a human. The amount known is an indicator of job performance

Figure 16.4 – Development Cost Composition

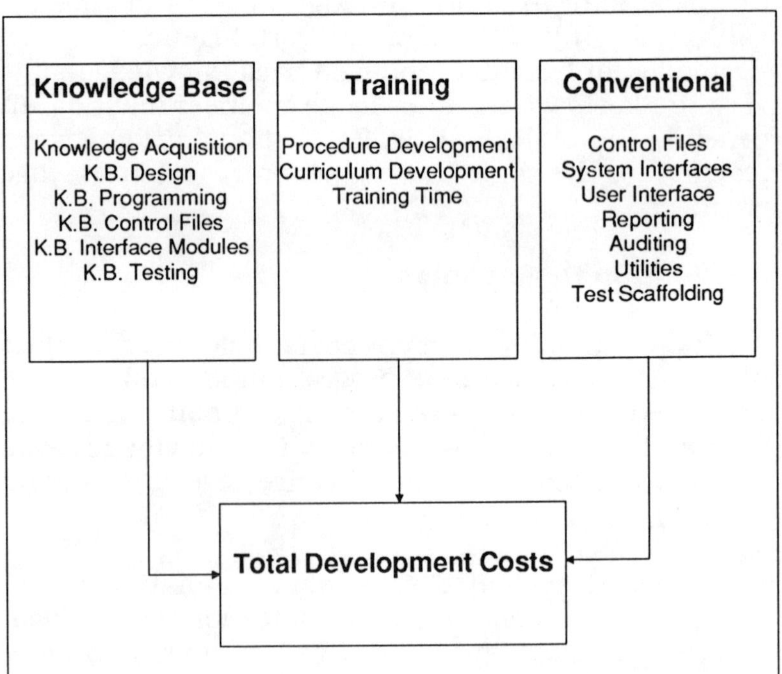

with performance increasing in direct proportion to new knowledge learned. As an organization learns, its new knowledge should be added to the knowledge base even if it is working properly. Maintenance of this type is an investment in the future, and prevents the organization from outgrowing the application. Even though the technical and staff time required to maintain a system can be substantial, most expert system projects miss this point because so much emphasis is placed on development and delivery.

There are also trade-offs to be made between development and maintenance costs that should be addressed during the planning phases. Extra time spent in development in design, testing, and developing support software can greatly reduce maintenance costs.

Figure 16.5 – Maintenance Costs

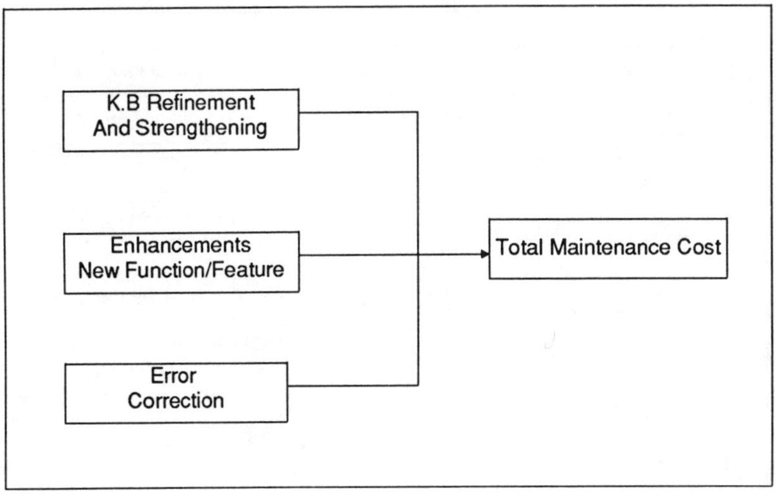

Benefits

Expert system benefits can be primary or secondary. Primary benefits arise solely from the consistency, quality, and control aspects of expert system applications. Conventional system components may be needed to implement the overall application and many of the secondary benefits stem from these conventional components. Both components provide benefits, but each magnifies or enables the benefits of the other.

Because of the interplay between primary and secondary benefits, benefit structures can become circular. For simplicity, this discussion outlines one possible benefit structure that ignores circularity.

Figure 16.6 – Expert System Benefit Structure

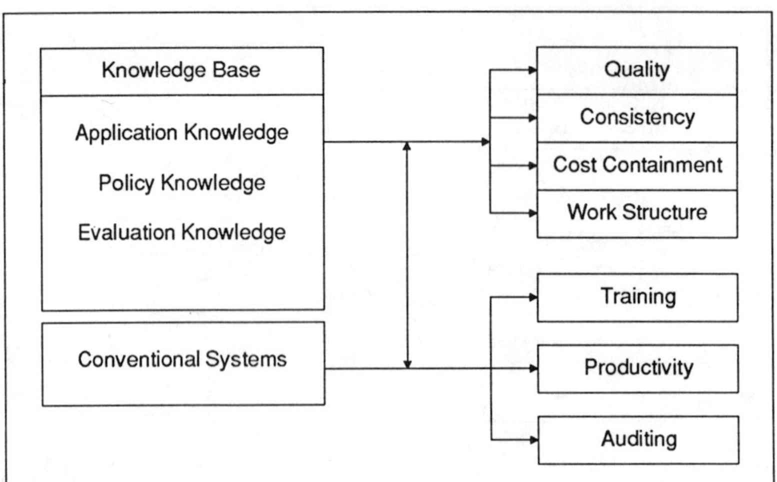

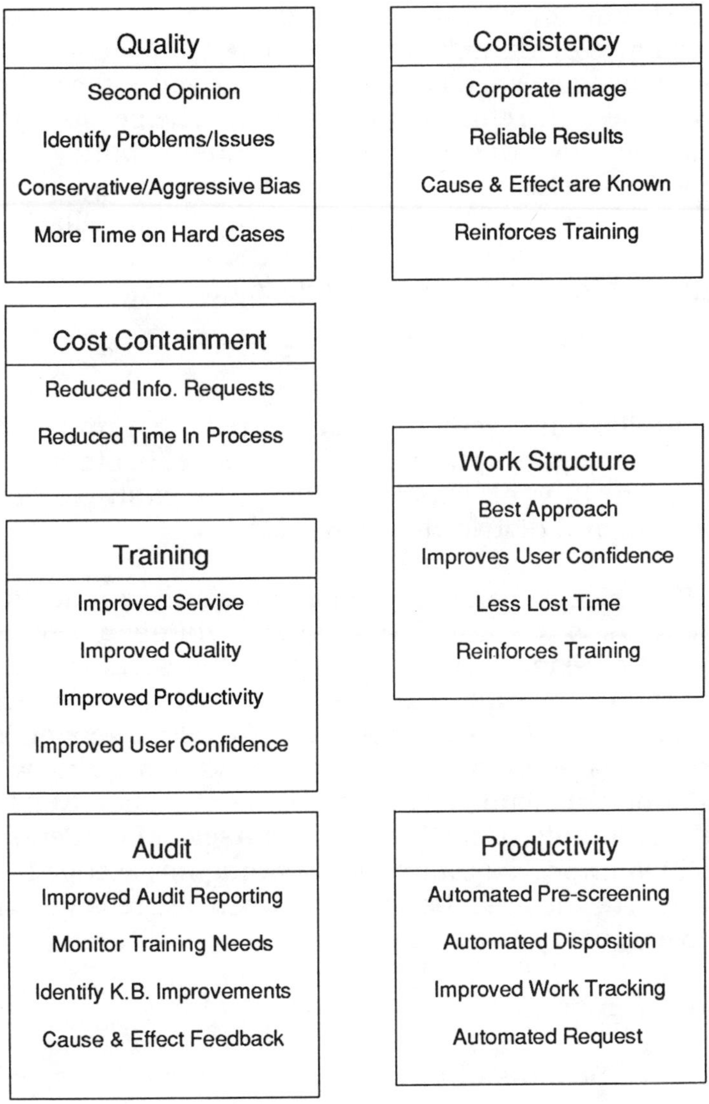

Figure 16.7 – Expert System Benefits

A knowledge base can be considered to contain three types of management-controlled knowledge. Application knowledge consists of facts and information about the nature of the application. The second type of knowledge describes management policy and guidelines. Decision and evaluation knowledge represents the intelligence of the system. The intelligence, or heuristic knowledge, governs the analysis process and how/when other knowledge is used.

Quality

Quality improvement is considered the number one benefit of expert systems. Quality benefits stem from the capability of expert systems to capture, concentrate, and distribute knowledge.

The expert system component of the application serves as a paraprofessional, providing a second opinion on each case. The application sorts through information, identifies issues, and provides guidance. Properly designed, the application focuses users on issues and shields them from time-consuming review of unimportant detail. This increases the effectiveness and the quality of analysis by the user. Management can also improve quality by providing knowledge that strikes the desired balance between aggressive and conservative decision making.

Consistency

Three benefits of any computer system are speed, reliability, and repeatability. Expert systems extend the reliability and repeatability of numeric procedural computer systems to the realm of the human decision process. Expert systems are capable of consistently guiding users in the application of management guidelines and philosophy. Uniformly presented, consistent decisions help improve the corporate image, fairness, or compliance.

Cost Containment

Cost containment is applicable where the user can elect to take some action that has a direct cost associated with it. In these situations, expert systems can help guide the user to the most appropriate action that will result in the lowest direct cost to the company.

Work Structure

Work structure, training, and productivity benefits are very closely related. Work structure can include a computerized proceduralization of the work flow enforced by conventional software components. It can also include guidance in structuring the decision/analysis or help users through unfamiliar procedures.

Training

Training benefits of expert systems are often overstated and underdelivered. Expert systems can provide substantial training benefits, but these benefits do not magically materialize as promised by the salesman. As was discussed in an earlier chapter, the explanation facilities provided in many development tools are only part of the answer. Depending on the application, additional development effort may be required to create user-friendly multi-level explanation facilities that support users with different experience levels.

Productivity

Productivity improvements flow from both the conventional and expert system components of the application. But with expert systems productivity can be a double-edged sword – some productivity may have to be given up in some areas to achieve productivity gains elsewhere. Additional data entry, changes in work flow, or additional dialogue with the computer may lower productivity at certain points, but depending on system design, productivity gains can be realized through decreased decision, auditing, and processing time especially if the system has semi-autonomous components.

Productivity improvement is often used as the primary justification for conventional computer systems and this practice has been transferred to expert systems. Using productivity as the primary justification for expert systems may be a case of using yesterday's yardstick to measure tomorrow's technology. In many cases, expert systems can be justified solely on the basis of improved decision/analysis or professional leveraging.

Auditing

It is not uncommon for expert systems to automate or support manual processes beyond the scope of conventional systems. Once the manual process comes under the automation umbrella, additional information becomes available. Conventional systems can report what happened, but they cannot report if it was what management wanted. Expert system capability enables functions capable of reporting both what and how well business was handled. Reporting of this type can not only improve the productivity of auditors, but can also improve the effectiveness of the auditing staff. In addition, the improved auditing and reporting capabilities, when used properly, allow management to identify needed training and knowledge base improvements.

Justification

Many companies are justifying expert system development strictly for strategic reasons. Some companies are justifying expert systems based on competitive or defensive arguments. Still others are justifying expert systems simply as a way to get a handle on key aspects of their business. Justification of expert systems for such strategic reasons is beyond the scope of this discussion; however, application-specific justification can be addressed.

One of the biggest problems in cost justifying an expert system is the apparent problem of quantifying the dollar value of improved quality, consistency, and control benefits that expert systems are supposed to provide. The first step in establishing this value is to determine the potential target of opportunity.

The methods for doing this have already been introduced. The confusion matrix can be used to measure average staff performance against expert performance. The 80/20 rule can be used to identify those areas that will provide the highest payback. Taken together, these two measures will yield the economic target of opportunity for expert system use. If there is little room for improvement, or if even substantial improvement would produce meager financial returns, the system will have to be justified using conventional measures such as productivity.

Since system development costs can be reasonably estimated, the amount of improvement needed in the confusion matrix index to cost justify the system can directly be determined. If the system can be reasonably expected (and this is a judgment call) to produce the required improvement, the system can be expected to be cost effective. The minimum improvement in the confusion matrix index becomes part of the contract between the technical staff and management as well as the least acceptable result for system testing and certification.

Figure 16.8 – Total Confusion Cost – Cost Times Frequency

	Best Recommendation			
Actual Decision	**Buy**	**Sell**	**Hold**	**Reevaluate**
Buy	0	1000	500	400
Sell	750	0	400	400
Hold	350	500	0	200
Reevaluate	300	300	80	0
Col. Totals	1400	1800	980	1000
Grand Total	5180			

Using the Confusion Matrix

The stock advisor system introduced in Chapter 14 is a good a example of confusion matrix usage. As a quick review, the confusion matrix rating for the existing staff is shown in Figure 16.8. The confusion matrix shows the average cost of errors for a representative sample of one-hundred test cases is $5,180. Since random distribution would produce a cost of $28,560 the confusion matrix rating was 81.9%. Another way to view Figure 16.8 is that on average each decision made costs the investment house $51.80.

$5,180 / 100 decisions

If we assume that each user will use the system once per hour and there will be ten users, then the total number of decisions per year would be 20,000.

10 users X 1 decision/hour X 2,000 hours/year

Based on these numbers, the total annual target of opportunity would be $1,036,000

$51.80/decision X 20,000 decisions

If the system would cost $250,000 to develop, and the investment house wanted to recoup its investment in one year, then the average cost per decision would have to be reduced by $12.50.

$250,000 / 20,000 decisions.

So, to recoup the investment the system would have to produce recommendations that result in a confusion matrix score of $3,930 or better.

($51.80/decision - $12.50/decision) X 100 decisions.

A score of $3,930 would yield a confusion matrix rating of 86.2% which is only a 4.3% improvement over current staff performance.

Business Payback

For those tasked with the responsibility of cost justifying new system development, usually the first reaction is to find a way to save money either by increasing productivity, or lowering training costs. Computer systems can be employed defensively to reduce tangible costs, or offensively to increase margins or sales without reducing production costs.

The confusion matrix example in the previous section is an example of the latter. A modest improvement in the quality of the decisions (4.3%) yielded a $250,000 annual return. In this hypothetical example, the largest target of economic opportunity is improving the quality of decisions. If we assumed the average personnel cost per user was $80,000, productivity would have to be increased by over 30% to yield an equivalent return. However, in our world of heavy conventional computer automation, most cost effective productivity gains have already been achieved.

Even though expert systems can improve productivity and lower training costs, the first place to look for business payback is in the area of intangibles: improved quality, consistency and control. As a society, we tend to be skeptical about new technologies. As long as the skepticism persists, expert systems will probably be used as assistant/mentor systems. Until we move past the imitative phase, autonomous systems, where the next major productivity gains lie, will be rare.

Double Returns

One concern companies have about expert systems is that employees will let the computer do the thinking for them. Case histories indicate this is not the case. Instead, the resulting computer-user combination results in performance better than either the computer or the user individually. The reasoning for this is as follows:

When both the user and the computer agree performance is not affected.

When the user has the right answer and the computer the wrong answer, the user usually prevails.

When the computer has the right answer and the user is wrong, the explanation facilities of the expert system generally persuade the user to change his position.

For example, if we use the confusion matrix example a pure random distribution of outcomes would be as follows:

> The user is right 81.9% of the time, and agrees with a correct computer response 86.2% of the time. Therefore, both agree on the correct answer 70.6% (.819 times .862) of the time.
>
> The user is right 81.9% of the time, and the computer is wrong 13.8% of the time. So, the user will be right 11.3% of the time when the computer is wrong.
>
> The user is wrong 18.1% of the time, and the computer right 86.2% of the time. So, the computer will be right 15.6% of the time when the user is wrong.
>
> Both the computer and the user will agree on the wrong answer on 2.5% of all cases.

If we assume that anytime there is a disagreement, the user will pick the correct answer 81.9% of the time, which is his current average, the resulting confusion matrix rating is computed in the table below.

Both Right				70.6%
Computer Right	15.6%	X	81.9%	12.8%
User Right	11.3%	X	81.9%	9.3%
Total Rating				92.7%

Similar results cannot be guaranteed, but even a small improvement (4.3%) contributed by an expert system can result in much larger gains (10.8%).